Experiences of Trance, Physical Mediumship

and
Associated Phenomena

<u>PART ONE</u>

Evidence of Survival After Death

written and compiled by

Katie Halliwell

Part One of a series of booklets with CDs.

Discover how we see, hear and touch the
Spirit People within the Alexander Circle

© The Stewart Alexander Circle & Katie Halliwell
2003, 2004, 2008

All rights of the owners reserved.
Except for brief quotations in critical articles or reviews,
no part of this book and the accompanying CDs may be
reproduced in any manner without prior written permission
of the author or publisher.

First Edition August 2003
Second Edition July 2004
Third Revised Edition 2008

Published by
Saturday Night Press Publications
York, England
snppbooks@yahoo.co.uk

Further copies of this book and the CD available from:-
The Alexander Project,
rjlister001@rjlister001.karoo.co.uk

ISBN-13 978-0-9514534-8-3

Printed by Lightning Source
www.lightningsource.com

Cover:- The Home Circle celebrate the launch of Katie's first book, Aug 2003

Dedicated to

White Feather, Walter Stinson,
Freda Johnson, Christopher
(the Spirit Team)
for their continuous love, patience
and devotion.

Appreciation

We would like to thank Ray and June Lister and their 'Home Circle' for all their help and support in making it possible for our Spirit friends to communicate with the public. Their continuous love and service is very much appreciated.

Also thanks must go to Tom and Ann Harrison for their constant help, advice and invaluable support and contribution towards the project.

Ann's work in transcribing all the audio sections, producing the CD and finally drawing it all together as publisher, is greatly appreciated.

The time and effort involved in producing this book and the accompanying CD has all been given voluntarily. We would like you to know that the proceeds above the cost of production will go to health and caring charities of Stewart's choice.

Special Note

If you have purchased this book without the CD
you can obtain it from:-
The Alexander Project,
rjlister001@rjlister001.karoo.co.uk

(see page 107 for details)

Conditions of Thought

It is important to be able to sit and listen to the silence of your thoughts, for that is your very own channel and entry into the Spirit World - **A World of Thought.**

Thought is creation whether it be negative or positive, and positive thought is extremely important when you sit in a Circle. Positive thought is open thought; it allows love, truth and goodness to flow through whenever you hold a séance.

You sit for the love of the Spirit World.

You sit for the beauty of natural harmony.

You sit for meditation and peace.

You sit to be of service to others.

You sit for the goodness and healing of life everlasting.

Let the light come in and never allow negative thoughts to enter.

Negative thoughts close the door to truth and harmony.

So listen to your own thoughts -

Are they positive or are they negative?

Negative thoughts are fear of the unknown -

Suspicions of any fraudulent activity or -

Selfish and wanting thoughts, expecting too much too soon.

So my dear reader, study your own thoughts carefully. Always think of your departed loved ones being happy and free in the World of Spirit. Give them your love and your thoughts will be open to them - **and do not expect -** this opposes the law of free will and the harmony is lost. Time does not exist in the Spirit World, so sit, be patient, be free in the Spirit World of Thought.

Listening to music can help bring the harmony you need, be your own, be at one, be unselfish and give, - give out loving feelings and bless your own consciousness, bless the beauty of your life, send out love, for love is light. Sincere unselfish love is an open door to those in the Spirit World.

Think seriously about your own thoughts for they are the result of your sitting. Be at peace with yourself.

From 'them upstairs' through Katie Halliwell

Stewart Alexander

Contents

Chapter		Page
1.	Introduction	11
2.	Foreword	13
3.	My Search for Truth	20
	Hull Séance Report, July 1999	32
4.	Read and Listen	37
	Introduction to Recordings	
	Sections 1 to 20	40
5.	Reports from i) America	50
	ii) Switzerland	55
	iii) England	63
6.	Audio Transcript	71

Introduction

I would like to share my séance room experiences of 1999 to 2001 with people willing to consider fairly and impartially the contents of this book (Part One) and the accompanying audio CD.

However these have not been produced in order to appeal to those with closed minds, or those who would approach the movement of Spiritualism out of idle curiosity and/or with overt scepticism.

People with concrete ideas that the Spirit people do not exist, unknowingly create a barrier for themselves and, in so doing, adversely affect the delicate emotional balance of the séance room so that the generation of physical phenomena and evidential communication often proves impossible.

Stewart Alexander is the trance and physical phenomena medium in whose circle I have had these experiences. It has taken him over 35 years to develop and even at this advanced stage he is still developing. As the Spirit team becomes stronger in using Stewart as an instrument, they increase the ability for our loved ones to be able to communicate with us.

The Spirit people will only come if they are invited to do so and because of the 'like attracts like' law of free will and service, patience with an open mind is, of course, very important.

When conditions were good within the séance room the manifesting phenomena was tangible, so much so that we all heard, saw and witnessed the same thing. In the darkness of the séance room Direct Voice occasionally manifested, as also did full materialisation.

You will also read and hear about my experiences involving ectoplasm by means of which we were all able to see and touch the materialised Spirit hand in the red light. In addition to such rare physical phenomena, experiments were conducted to demonstrate the passage of solid inanimate matter through living matter; séance room trumpets* regularly moved around in mid air; and self-illuminated lights sometimes appeared in the room, both pin-sized and large diffused masses. Believe me, there was most certainly no fraud involved in these wonders.

It has been my single hope and intention that this work, and all that has been recorded herein, will be of service and will offer evidence of a life eternal to anyone willing to consider what follows with intelligence, with sincerity and with love.

Thank you.

Katie

---

* *(See 'General Comment' on page 43 for description).*

Foreword

First of all I would like to congratulate Katie Halliwell on the production of this book, and the accompanying recording.

When first she mentioned it to me back in the summer of 1999, I failed then to fully appreciate its potential value to people everywhere. Particularly those who had an interest in life beyond death and mediumistic communication between the two worlds.

However, her determination to push ahead with the project has, in my opinion, resulted in this easy to understand work, which it is hoped will make clear much about Spiritualism which hitherto has been bathed in confusion.

As we know, there have long existed within the Spiritualist movement, profound teachings both in book and audio form, transmitted from the Spirit World through a number of excellent mediums.

Such information, on many aspects of Spiritualism, has been delivered over the past 150 years, often with considerable eloquence, and this stands as a permanent record and testimony to the wisdom and compassion of the other world.

However, although this is very clearly recognised, I have long taken the view that such valuable transmissions can lead to confusion in the minds of people new to the teachings of the movement.

This I firmly believe, is where this work will prove to be of particular service for it will inform the listener, in straightforward easy to understand language, about matters which previously have been open to misunderstanding and misinterpretation.

The communicators you will hear on the accompanying CD speak directly about their own understanding of trance and physical mediumship but it is for you the listener to decide what you can and cannot accept.

They, our Spirit friends, do not profess or insist that they possess the absolute truth about the subjects they speak on but 35 years' association with them has convinced me that they always speak in total conviction and with sincerity.

And, of course, their own vision is considerably more elevated than our own.

My development as a trance and physical medium extends back over 35 years, during which time my circle and I have been highly privileged to regard our Spirit visitors as cherished ever dependable friends.

Always, their message of survival beyond death has been given with compassion and love and always it has been given with consistency of fact.

Throughout those years I have developed my gifts within the privacy of my own séance room together with family and friends - week by week, month by month and year by year.

In that environment and atmosphere of absolute harmony, the gifts of the Spirit gradually unfolded and we were privileged to witness the wonders of the communication between the two worlds on a physical level which, in today's world, is extremely rare.

Truly, that small room gradually became a very real meeting place between the two worlds and remains so to the present day.

Then, in the early 1990's, we decided to share what we had with the Spiritualist community and in taking it to the outside world I was to travel, together with other circle members, throughout England, Scotland and Switzerland.

Additionally, we held a special Guest Circle each week so that people had the opportunity to witness, in our small séance room, 'The Great Reality' - and it was in one of those that I first met Katie.

Such public work led to thousands of people attending my séances and our Spirit friends took those opportunities to transmit their wonderful message of survival and direct communication.

From time to time, in addition to the production of phenomena, reunions would take place where the living were able to communicate with their loved ones beyond the grave. These were very precious moments.

In general, the mass public séances were very successful in spite of the fact that often the conditions we expected our Spirit friends to work within were far from balanced and ideal. This, therefore, was quite a remarkable achievement. However, on occasions - although they always managed to communicate - it was very evident that the channel between the two worlds was far from clear yet even then, one would admire their considerable effort not to disappoint.

The miracle is, of course, not so much in the nature of what they communicated but, the fact that they could communicate at all in extremely difficult circumstances. When the channel was unclear, the communications also became unclear - in much the same way as the conversation between two parties on a telephone line suffers when the connection has developed a fault. Yet even on such occasions as those they did their best.

Throughout those years of public work, our Spirit friends repeatedly emphasised that their mission was not to present us with complex philosophical teachings - they were quite happy to leave that to elevated souls working through other mediums.

Always, it was maintained that the production of physical phenomena had to take prominence above all else.

Repeatedly, they told us that it was of considerable importance that people should have the opportunity to experience for themselves what, today, is a unique form of mediumship.

Sadly, during this past half century, this has almost disappeared from our world and yet - 150 years earlier, the movement was built and established upon it.

Our public séances became a balance between the production of physical phenomena and personal evidential communication.

Phenomena alone will not, and does not, prove the survival of the human soul beyond death - that is why evidence was, and always will be of paramount importance. Over the years, we witnessed many a reunion between the living and the so-called 'dead' at our séances and we had the fulfilling satisfaction of knowing that often, people left the séances assured death is but the gateway to a larger life.

But perhaps our most valued and cherished experience was in the ever-present love, friendship and understanding support which, at all times, permeated the very fabric of our small 'Home Circle' séance room.

In January 2001, following ten years of working before the public, I finally took the decision to cancel all my future public work, and retire back into the safety of my Home Circle.

Although many people are bound to speculate as to the reason behind that decision, it is really quite simple. A physical medium demonstrating in public outside of the security of his/her home circle, takes a considerable risk concerning their well-being and must implicitly trust everyone present not to break the conditions of the séance room.

However, it is a sad fact that, even amongst Spiritualists, there exists considerable ignorance concerning the mechanics behind such mediumship, and ignorance also concerning the potential inherent dangers involved with such demonstrations.

Additionally, I personally take the view that there are two faces to the Spiritualist movement.

Firstly, there exists the public face, and secondly there exists a form whereby communication with the Spirit World is achieved quietly outside of, and away from, the public arena, totally unknown to the outside world. Since I am largely a private individual, the public form has never sat easily with me because I have never knowingly invited any manner of public notoriety.

What I did was for the Spirit World, and for people in need of the kind of comfort that can only be derived from the séance room.

Additionally, ten years of pressure, descending upon me from many directions, was more than enough, and I considered that I had done my duty and my best for the Spirit people, and for the Movement of Spiritualism.

As I write these words I am aware (and have always been aware) that physical mediumship lends itself to constant suspicion, and often accusations of fraud, and this is because the phenomena manifests within the dark séance room, because the essential extracted energy (Ectoplasm) is extremely sensitive to any form of light - natural or artificial.

As a direct result of this, controversy has always surrounded such mediumship, and throughout the history of modern Spiritualism many accusations of fraud have been made.

Sometimes such exposures have proved justified but

occasionally they have merely demonstrated the rank ignorance of the accusers.

The disgraceful circumstances surrounding the wicked so-called exposure and treatment of the materialisation medium Helen Duncan back in the 1950's was one such case.

From a personal point of view I have long believed that critics of physical mediumship really ought to appreciate its complexities - its nature, and the mechanics which lie behind it.

To cry 'fraud' is a simple matter - anyone can do so. What is required urgently is for a programme of education to be launched by the Spiritualist Movement concerning all its various facets and aspects, so that people can become advised and informed. After all - how, in the name of common sense, can we expect people with little or no knowledge about the subject, to accept that the so-called dead can physically manifest within our séance rooms, when conditions are correct and a suitable medium is present.

Quite simply we cannot.

Physical mediumship - once the jewel in the crown of Spiritualism, is in grave danger of dying away.

Surrounded as it is by a lack of understanding in the modern world in which we live - perhaps it is even now too late, and it will become extinct in the near future.

Perhaps I am simply pessimistic - I hope so.

Before closing, I would like to assure all readers and listeners of this work that my long, intimate experience within the séance room has left me in no doubt whatsoever that truly life is eternal.

There is no death, only continuous life, and under certain conditions the so-called dead can, and do communicate with us.

Finally, I am more than happy to regard this book and CD

as a permanent record of my work as a medium, and I thank Katie Halliwell for her vision and industry. Additionally I would like to take this opportunity to thank all the members of my Home Circle who have been ever present at my side for so many years.

And last but not least I thank my principal communicators:- White Feather - Walter Stinson - Christopher - Freda Johnson and also the many unseen workers who stand behind them, for their years of hard work, for their love and loyalty, and for their valued friendship. It has been a privilege working for them.

Stewart Alexander
January 2002

<u>Addendum</u>
(In May 2003), due to public demand Stewart Alexander decided to give a further limited number of public séances.

My Search for Truth

Because people have asked me so many questions regarding my experiences, I decided to put some of them together into a package in the hope of giving a broader outlook of the truth as I believe it to be. Also because so many people have asked me 'Katie, why Spiritualism?' I feel it may help to include a brief story of my life to explain how and why I became involved in Spiritualism. And how that led to my first visit to the Alexander Circle which brought me into contact with the wonderful souls from the Spirit World .

In The Beginning

As a child, I used to hop onto a double-decker bus and race upstairs to get to the front seat so I could use my imagination and pretend I was flying a craft a few feet above the ground. Yes! My imagination was strong and I enjoyed playing pilot, but I can remember how my happy playful thoughts were often disturbed whenever we would drive past a graveyard. I was often puzzled at the sight of those cold, dark, heavy gravestones which led me to the question almost every child asks: "Why do we die and what happens to us then?".

Of course, I never got a straightforward answer, but was happy to go along with what I was told, "You go to heaven but if you are bad you go to hell".

It didn't stop me wondering why life existed. I continued to ask myself questions throughout my teenage years, such as:- 'Why are we here and where is this Heaven and Hell? Why do children suffer? Why is there so much violence in our World? Why are there so many different religions and yet there is only one God?" I was definitely a seeker, looking for fact and reason. I investigated different religions, read the Bible from beginning to end, visited various different denominations, but still I found myself querying the mystery of life and death.

As an artist, I saw beauty in anything natural. I would absorb colours with such delight and I loved to concentrate on any flower, appreciating its very existence and delicacy. I found colours wonderful and relaxing and despite my deafness, I loved to listen to classical music. I was born partially deaf, and was educated at Odsal House School for the Deaf in Bradford. Later in life, I became a student at the Bradford College of Art which prepared me for a career as a Typographic Designer.

It was when I was 26 years old that my spiritual quest began. My mother became seriously ill with cancer, she was reduced to skin and bone and suffered a great deal and my emotional prayers poured out. I believed in God and begged him to release her from the living hell she was going through. She died on 20th October 1976. At first, I felt a great relief and then I felt horribly upset, wondering where I had sent her, what had my prayers done and where had she gone. Oh! I only hoped she was alright.

It was nine days after Mum died, the funeral had been and gone and things were beginning to settle down. Dad was worn out and my sister Christine suggested that he go back home with her to Sidcup in Kent for a few days. Dad deserved a much needed rest and a break . Although he and Christine were concerned about leaving me, I encouraged him to go, and since I had to go to work anyway, I wouldn't be alone all the time. When I came home from work that day, I had a very strong feeling that Mum was around. What happened that evening was something I will never forget.

I went to bed and when I set the alarm clock I noticed it was 10.15 p.m. I slipped under the covers, turned off the light, closed my eyes and lay there hoping Mum was alright. I remember two words came loud and clear into my mind, "Concentrate, Concentrate". I felt as if I was receiving some kind of instruction then I physically felt a cold, short blast of air at the back of my head. Immediately after it Mum's face appeared before me in full colour, clear and vivid. She was younger and wearing the blue spiked glasses she had worn about 20 years before. More to the point, she was smiling and happy. I instantly sat up and felt total peace. It was then, I knew she was alright. I looked at the clock and it was only 10.30 p.m. The vision I had had was definitely no dream nor a figment of my imagination.

That cold, short blast at the back of my head was felt with such force and there was definitely no draught in the room. From then on, as the years went by, I started to look towards Spiritualism.

The Healing Years

Although I started to think about Spiritualism, I hadn't the courage to investigate it seriously. I was frightened, very frightened, of the unknown and I had a fear of becoming possessed by some kind of unwanted entity.

My only direct experience of dabbling with, should I say, psychism, was in the late sixties when I had a go at the glass on the table with the letters of the alphabet placed in a circle. Four of us sat round this table, Mum, Dad, Christine and myself, (we were a happy close loving family - Dad loved to joke and Mum loved to tease in a happy social way). It wasn't long before Dad was banished from the table for purposely moving the glass, but later, Mum's chuckling face suddenly turned serious. She shrieked and said, "I'm having nothing to do with this" and hurried away from the table. Christine and I asked what was wrong, "It's your Little Grandma", Mum blurted out, "She used to chase me and say, I'm after your XYZ". Chris and I, realising the glass had spelt out the last three letters of the alphabet, looked at each other and dismantled everything on the table, purely because of fear on our part. We never tried it again.

My tentative entry into Spiritualism really started in the eighties.

Dad had now remarried and was very happy living in Eldwick with my stepmum, Myra. I was still living in Halifax and working at a printing company in Elland as a typographic designer. In my spare time I loved to try anything new, so my hobbies were quite varied; Swimming, Badminton, Yoga, Computer Studies, etc. One of my interests was Homeopathy and I became very friendly with a Homeopathic Consultant called Angela Clark. I helped to form the local Homeopathic Society and I often found my feet under the table at Angela's place. One day whilst having tea, the subject of Spiritual Healing came up and it turned out that Angela's husband, John, was a Spiritual Healer, he didn't take any money and it was all done in his spare time. I was intrigued by this and asked him if he could have a go at my deafness.

Deep down inside me, I was still affected by that wonderful experience of seeing Mum after she died, but still afraid of Spiritualism. Doris Stokes came to the Halifax Civic Theatre, I thought about going, but didn't. John's Spiritual Healing seemed safe enough and at my request he gave me hands-on healing as often as he could. When John found out that I had a sister living in Guildford, he recommended that I visited the Harry Edwards Healing Sanctuary which is near Guildford.

On my next trip to Christine's for a holiday, I told her I would like to visit the Harry Edwards Healing Sanctuary. Christine, being very concerned and worried, decided to come with me. It was a lovely place, very peaceful and we certainly had nothing to fear as I took healing from Ray and Joan Branch. Afterwards, as Christine and I had cream teas at Gomshall, Christine looked at me and said, "Well, can you hear?". I said, "Pardon?". We then looked at each other and started to laugh. I made two more trips later on and continued with absent healing for a time, but my deafness was not alleviated. But strangely enough, something else was - my fear of Spiritualism.

Coming home from Christine's, the coach broke down on the M1 and I started reading a Spiritualist magazine which I had picked up at the Sanctuary. Two ladies who were sitting on the seat behind me leaned over and asked, "Are you into all that stuff?" They made me jump and I didn't know what to say. "Well, kind of, yes", I replied. The two ladies started talking about Spiritualist churches and recommended the Huddersfield church. They told me it was behind the Sports Centre and I should try it, I didn't have to be a member and I could go any Sunday.

Well, I had visited many different churches seeking for fact and reason, but here was one I hadn't checked out. I had a very strong urge to go.

The Doorway

You know that awful feeling when you are entering some-where strange and your head goes through the door before your feet do? Well, mine did and there I was in the Huddersfield Spiritualist Church. I was greeted very warmly by a man called Harold. He gave me a song book and showed me the way in. The first thing that struck me was that it was full. I managed to find a spare seat and I noticed some people were standing. I sat down and looked around, - nothing spooky about this place! What I had been expecting I had no idea. The organist played happy, cheerful music; the people were chatting away; the atmosphere was very relaxed indeed. The lady sitting next to me started chatting and I told her it was my first time in a Spiritualist church, "Oh!", she said, "You'll like it, we start off with prayers and songs then we have philosophy, then communication with the Spirit people, after that we go in there for tea and biscuits and a natter."

What really fascinated me was that the philosophy came from the heart of the speaker and not from a book. There was nothing contrived here and everything was spoken with genuine intent, whether you agreed with what was said it was down to you to accept it or not. The medium then relayed messages from the Spirit World to various people and I found out that they had different mediums every week from all over the country, so you weren't stuck with the same old speaker.

I liked it and started to go to Huddersfield Spiritualist church most Sundays. I also discovered that there was a Spiritualist church in Sowerby Bridge, not far from where I live.

Sunday 24th September 1989 saw my first visit to this smaller church and I sat next to a lady, a complete stranger until we got talking and introduced ourselves. The lady was called Joan, and after the service I offered her a lift home. She invited me in for coffee and when I walked into her room I saw some excellent psychic drawings hung up on the wall. Joan told me the name of the artist who lived in Sheffield, and if I was interested, I could write to him and send a passport photograph of myself for the psychic artist to meditate on.

I decided to try that, but I was not happy about sending a passport photograph. I didn't want the artist to pick out any particular facial features giving him the opportunity to make the drawings look like my family members so I sent him this photograph instead and as you can see my face is small enough to alleviate any possible cheating.

The letter and photograph were posted on Thursday 28th September.

The photograph Katie sent to the psychic artist

On Sunday 1st October, I went to the Huddersfield Spiritualist church and was given my very first message.

I would like to point out that at this stage I was very keen to test the medium and would refuse to answer any questions the medium should ask, simply because I did not want to give away any hints, clues or even body language the medium could pick up on. that was the way I thought in those days, I fully expected the Spirit people to inform the medium of anything he needed to know.

The visiting platform medium who came from Rotherham looked at me and said, "I'm coming to you first because since the service began, the Spirit people have been eager to give you this message".

"Look at the photographs and you will see the picture".

The medium then gave me a quizzical look and said, "Does

27

that mean anything to you?"

I replied, "No".

The medium hesitated, then said, "That message is very important and it will mean something to you later on. Now I must move on to somebody else".

It was a very short message indeed and I was not impressed. In actual truth I had lied to the medium by saying no because I wanted him to tell me why he was giving me that message and I had expected the Spirit people to inform the medium as to why it was so important. But to be honest with you, I do remember that when the medium delivered that message, in the same instant he delivered it, I had a flash thought of psychic drawings and if my thought conditions had been what they are now, I would have cooperated.

That message actually caused me to immediately think of psychic drawings, and the communication was based on thought and thought energy is fast. Like many first timers in a Spiritualist church, I chose to communicate using the logic of my brain and not through the mind using thought energy.

On Wednesday 4th October I received three pencil drawings through the post from the psychic artist in Sheffield. In those days the post would come before I set off for work. I took one look at these drawings, expecting to see Mum or Grandma but I did not recognise anybody. Feeling disappointed, I threw the drawings on to the table and went to work.

As I was driving to work, I suddenly remembered the message - 'Look at the photographs and you will see the picture' so when I got home that same evening, I looked through a box of photographs and found three people of similar likeness.

The only drawing I could not really match up was (A). The nearest likeness I could find was Photograph 1. The gentleman in the drawing has a shorter chin and is not wearing spectacles. Some people thought it was the same person, but I was not at all convinced. The photograph is of Uncle H. and he is a blood relative.

A

1

The other two drawings, I was happy to accept. The drawing of the lady (B), matches with Auntie V. (photograph 2), and

B

2

the third drawing (C) matches with Uncle A. (photograph 3). Uncle A. was a friend of the family and a neighbour. I must have been about 9 years old when this gentleman passed to

C   3

Spirit and I had completely forgotten what he looked like.

I do remember these people and I was close to them, but they were not in my mind when I saw the drawings, simply because I had not seen them for such a long time.

If the psychic artist from Sheffield had been given the photographs of Auntie V. and Uncle A. to copy, I don't think he could have done much better. I was staggered. This really was spooky and what was even more so, was that it had been backed up by the message at Huddersfield church from a different medium, another stranger, from Rotherham.

What happened proved to me that no telepathy or mind reading had taken place when I was given the message because I wasn't even thinking of the people and I was convinced that the connection with the two separate mediums was definitely no coincidence.

I continued to go to Huddersfield church and was a member for over a year. I had several private sittings with various mediums which brought some good, interesting results.

We had Spirit communication with clairvoyant and clairaudient mediums on the platform. The majority were good, but I did come across some who were very manipulative with words and they did not appeal to me at all. I enjoyed the discussion group meetings and this gave me the chance to go back to my basic questions from my early days. The discussion group brought me into contact with a couple called Mr and Mrs Brake and little did I know then, that this was the start of a beautiful and close friendship.

Through the doorway

Georgina and Robert Brake invited me into their home. Ena and Bob, as I now know them, had moved up to Huddersfield not long before I walked into the Huddersfield church. There was something special about Ena & Bob. Somehow, they could answer my questions and they had a vast knowledge of Spiritualism.

I'll never forget the first time I walked into their house. It was like going into a library; they had books everywhere. To me it was like Aladdin's Cave, with everything I needed to know: life stories of mediums, writings of Silver Birch, Yogi Ramacharaka, The Rosicrucians, White Eagle Lodge, Red Cloud etc, etc. I had studied various religions and organisations before, but this was like walking into a different sphere on Earth.

There was a lovely atmosphere about their home and I spent many a happy time there borrowing and returning the books. What fascinated me was their knowledge and experience of physical mediumship, they talked about Direct Voice and Ectoplasm, 'Trumpets' moving in the air, Apports etc. and they had actually sat with the legendary Helen Duncan.

I continued to visit the Huddersfield Spiritualist church until Dad became very ill. He had cancer and there were frequent visits to Cookridge Hospital. By the end of 1990, he had been taken into Manorlands Hospice and stayed there until he passed away on 20 April 1991. Much of my time was spent travelling over to Bingley and Oxenhope, but I still visited Bob and Ena and borrowed their books.

Manorlands Hospice did so much to help Dad, I was fascinated by the care they gave to the patients and became a voluntary worker there. I had already got to know the patients as I used to sit in the lounge chatting to them when I visited Dad and so continued to visit them after Dad died. I took part in the bereavement support group, served tea and drinks to the patients and visitors and helped with the charity garden parties, etc. I also helped in the day care room showing patients how to draw and paint pictures.

In 1992 I was made redundant, but I continued to work part time at Manorlands until I left for a full time job in Bradford as an administrative assistant in 1993. I spent many happy weekends with my stepmum, Myra. We went on short trips everywhere and on holidays together. Due to family commitments I had, by now, stopped going to the Huddersfield church, but I kept in close contact with Bob and Ena.

The Noah's Ark Society for Physical Mediumship was to be my next step. I became a member and received their interesting journals. I was not an active member for a while, but it was interesting to read about various circles all over the country developing the physical phenomena Bob and Ena so often talked about.

Ena had handwritten four copies of a book about her life story which were to be distributed to her family and she invited me to read one of them. I was so impressed that I offered to type it out so that it could be printed and sent to many of Ena's friends. What happened with Ena's book is a story in itself. It was so well liked and has helped so many people.

Because I had read and heard so much about Direct Voice and Ectoplasm and helped to print a book about it, I developed the urge to seek out the real thing. Listening to Bob and Ena was very interesting, but I felt I really needed to experience such phenomena for myself.

Through the Noah's Ark Society I plucked up the courage to go to my first séance. It was so amazing that I wrote a report about the evening which was published in the Society's Journal and I'd like to share it with you here.

Hull Séance Report, 8th July,1999

The time is 10am on 9th July 1999. I am sitting in a picnic area, glancing over the pond at Burton Agnes in East Yorkshire. To the left of me is Burton Agnes Hall around which I am going to venture later.

There is a lovely cool breeze and today is a day of my holidays, but today is very special. I write these notes with a feeling of elation and tears in my eyes, tears of happiness, that so many people deprive themselves of.

For many years, I have had the sense of life after death. I have visited Spiritualist Churches, had private sittings with various mediums; have often read about contact with Spirit through Direct Voice and materialisation and many, many times have my dear friends Ena and Bob (Georgina and Robert Brake), told me of their wonderful experiences with Direct Voice and ectoplasm. I believed this was true and it was wonderful to believe, but now, there is no need to believe! I had actually seen and heard the real thing! Just as real as the pond and trees I am looking at now. What happened last night was something I will never forget!

Earlier this year, I had booked a place in a home circle through the Noah's Ark Society. The medium was Mr Stewart Alexander. I had never been to a physical phenomena circle before but I knew I had to sit in the dark. I wasn't nervous, but quite apprehensive with a certain air of excitement. I had that urge to investigate something I had only read about in books and heard about through hearsay.

Now was the opportunity to experience it personally.

One point I would like to mention to whomever is reading this report is, that I am very hard of hearing and I was quite concerned about not being able to hear the Spirit voices in the dark. I knew lip-reading would be totally impossible but really, I had nothing whatsoever to fear!!

Yesterday afternoon, I arrived at the hotel in Hull, and after a wash and something to eat I rang the circle leader, Ray Lister, to tell him I had arrived. Ray picked me up at 6.30, and his lovely, warm hearted, happy personality put me at ease straight away. I was taken to his house where the séance was to take place and I was introduced to the other circle members. We chatted for a while, but as I could not pick up group conversation, I was wondering how I would manage in the séance. I turned to Ray and said I was concerned about not being able to hear properly but Ray told me not to worry, as he would be sitting next to me and he would interpret for me if necessary.

Ray took me up the stairs into the séance room and showed me the corner where Stewart would be sitting. The room was painted black and chairs were positioned in a circle round a small table. On this table were two slim funnel-like objects with luminous tape stuck round the wider ends. Ray explained that these were the 'trumpets' our Spirit friends might use. I also saw two drumsticks and a bell.

Ray explained that Stewart would be fastened to the chair with plastic cable ties which cannot be broken. While Ray was talking, I had hold of one of these cable ties and started to fumble with it, I formed a loop and it automatically locked itself, once I had done this, there was no way I could loosen it. I apologised to Ray as I knew the cable tie would be no use now. Ray said, "That's no problem, we have plenty more", and I certainly knew why we would have to cut the medium loose

34

at the end of the séance.

Ray showed me where I would be sitting and he told me that if I did get frightened in the dark, I could grab his hand for reassurance. I went back downstairs and met Stewart who had a very loving and very warm personality.

At 8pm we all went up to the séance room. Stewart was strapped firmly to the chair and I noticed that two little luminous tabs were taped to his knees. The lights were switched off, but I wasn't really in total darkness, I could see the luminous paint on the edge of the trumpets and the two tabs on Stewart's knees. I concentrated on the luminous paint to eliminate the darkness, and I was entirely satisfied that no way could anyone move around without bumping into things.

A member of the circle opened up in prayer and soft music was played to lighten the atmosphere, then in just a few minutes, a North American Indian's voice came through, he seemed to be speaking from mid air, it was very clear and loud enough for me to hear. It was White Feather giving us his blessing and protection. I commented to Ray that I heard the Spirit voice very clearly and I was amazed at how loud it came over. Ray replied, saying, "He's the quiet one!"

Then a child's voice came through. This was Christopher, a loving, cheerful, laughing soul, who put us all at ease straight away. Tears of happiness started to form in my eyes as I actually heard a Spirit voice and I now knew it was true. The atmosphere was filled with nothing but unconditional love. Christopher's job was to relax people, especially the new- comers, and what a good job he did too! He was excellent and all my apprehension just simply faded away.

Christopher asked to be introduced to everyone and Ray introduced me first as I was sat next to him. After Christopher, Freda, another Spirit communicator, spent some time speaking to various people, then we were asked to play some music and one trumpet moved slowly into the air and then the other one moved as well. The two trumpets moved around above us and one reached up to the ceiling, the other made extremely quick rapid movements from one sitter to the next across the room. One of the trumpets slowed down and came towards me. Ray remarked that it was looking at me and I said "Yes it is", and then the trumpet slowly and directly touched my left arm and then very gently stroked my arm up and down. I also heard the drumsticks banging and the bell ringing.

Walter, another member of the Spirit team, who is responsible for producing all the physical phenomena, then came through and asked for the table to be moved up to the medium's knees. He then asked me to sit up to the table facing the medium. I couldn't see in the dark and Ray had to lead me up to the table and he brought my chair up to me. There was a red light shining through the table top and Walter asked for the intensity of the light to be lowered.

I then saw the ectoplasm roll onto the table, it looked like some kind of thick paste, a kind of mist rolling onto the table, some of it was transparent. I was asked to place my right hand, palm down, onto the table and keep it there perfectly still. I felt very privileged to witness this ectoplasm, and when it stopped rolling towards my hand, I saw one finger form out of this somewhat transparent substance, then a thumb appeared and another finger, until there was a fully materialised hand on the table. It was Walter's hand and it moved until it was above my hand and then it touched my fingers and stroked the back of my hand and fingers. I expected the ectoplasm to be wet, cold and slimy, but to my surprise it wasn't, it felt like a real hand, it certainly looked like a real hand, and it felt warm.

I came away from that séance feeling wonderfully elated, to have actually experienced the physical phenomena Ena and Bob had so often talked about. I also felt very privileged to have been physically touched by Walter's hand; to be touched by a soul from the Spirit World.

I close this report emphasising the extreme love the Spirit people expressed and the care and consideration they had for my hearing deficiency. The circle members too, were also extremely helpful, so, -- just a little word to anyone who is hard of hearing, "Don't ever let your hearing deficiency stop you from attending a circle".

White Feather, Christopher, Freda and Walter were the main Spirit contacts throughout the séance and a lot of interesting subjects were discussed.   *(end of report)*

Understandably, from time to time my associates, friends and family have questioned the role of imagination in respect of my séance reports.

However, through the mediumship of Stewart Alexander the reality of survival and communication has been demonstrated to a countless number of people over a great many years and they surely cannot all be wrong. Our Spirit friends communicate within the séance room in sincerity and in love, constantly urging that we should take our knowledge of survival out into the world, for it truly belongs to the whole of mankind.

Read and Listen to our Experiences

(with accompanying CD)

For readers unfamiliar with the mechanics of trance, I offer this very brief explanation. Usually the condition is achieved through meditation and results in a disconnection or dissociation of the mind (spiritual), from the brain (physical). This allows an external consciousness (Spirit), to take control of the medium's brain and therefore the organs of speech. However, this temporary connection may vary enormously from a light overshadowing, which exerts influence upon the medium's thoughts, to a deep state of absolute unconsciousness during which he/she is unaware of all that takes place. Although Stewart's mediumship is of the latter kind, we know from Spirit that the level of control achieved is never absolute. Transmissions are influenced by his own subconscious in a manner that we are unable to understand. However, in spite of that, the Spirit people generally achieve between 75 and 90% accuracy with their communications. Occasionally we observe them to repeat something they have just said, but in a different manner, so that the meaning is changed. Obviously, the original has been corrupted during the process of transmission.

Before we continue, I would like to outline the conditions under which the séances were conducted, as all sittings were in complete darkness at the request of the Spirit team.

Stewart always recognised the fact that people taking part in his public séances understandably needed the reassurance that the phenomena which developed owed nothing to his own conscious or unconscious actions. As a result he never sat for the public unless the following controls etc. were applied:

Immediately prior to a public séance he was often bodily searched to ensure that he took nothing into the room that could be used to create fraudulent activity.

He sat in his own high backed chair with wooden arms, and this was often closely examined by carpenters to ensure that there was nothing hidden within it which could be used fraudulently.

When the medium took his place his ankles, thighs and chest were all roped tightly to the chair and luminous tape was secured to his knees so that his exact position in the darkness of the séance room could be determined at all times. Needless to say - he never left his chair.

Strong electrical straps were then used to tightly secure his arms directly to the arms of the chair. Since these were self-locking, they could only be removed at the conclusion of a séance by the use of wire cutters.

Once secured, a representative of the sitters, as selected by them, came forward and checked all ties. He/she repeated this at the conclusion of the séance to ensure that all was as before.

Since Stewart always sat as a part of the circle his hands were often held by the sitters who occupied the seats at either side of him.

It is worth recording here that Stewart occasionally came out of trance when the phenomena was in progress, and he observed what was taking place at a distance from him. Occasionally this also extended to his actually hearing the direct voices which spoke independent of him.

And finally, on one occasion the sitter who occupied the seat on his left was asked to reach out and hold his hand, which she did. Interestingly, this took place at exactly the same time that a fully materialised form was standing directly in front of her, with hands resting lightly upon her head

When we hold a séance we need to create a happy, lively atmosphere in the room. We do this by playing music or singing and with happy chatter between circle members; sometimes the Spirit people also join in. However, I soon realised that friends who listened to the recordings did not always appreciate what was happening. It also became apparent that many people did not know anything about the trance state - what it is and how it works. This discovery prompted me to record snippets of the highlights on tape and paper, explaining what happened, what I saw and what I felt.

It may appear hard to believe but people who listened to the recordings made at various séances found it difficult to differentiate a Spirit person from a member of the circle. Yes...the communication was so good we actually talked to the Spirit person just as we talk to each other on this Earth plane.

So what you are about to read and listen to is real and true and on the accompanying CD you will hear our communication with the Spirit people through the trance and physical mediumship of Stewart Alexander. You will remember that I said I am quite deaf in both ears and can hear very little sound without hearing aids. Because I could not lip-read in the darkness of the séance room, you will notice how the Spirit people often made sure I was able to hear them. The circle members were also very helpful in repeating certain words for me.

I have divided the CD into a series of sections to take you through a step by step guide explaining the different experiments carried out in our physical phenomena séance, starting with trance communication through to full materialisation, at the same time, providing evidence of survival after death. Seven different recordings were used to produce this CD and so the sound fluctuates in the various sections.

I now ask you to read Section 1 which follows this, and then listen to Track 1 on the CD or read the transcript of

Track 1 on page 72. Before listening to each of the other tracks please refer back to the appropriate introductory section between pages 40 and 49; the track number and the page of the corresponding transcript are indicated at the end of each introductory section.

Introductions to the Recordings

Section 1 — Private sitting - 25th May 2000.
Stewart Alexander.

The first voice you will hear is that of our medium Stewart Alexander immediately upon his return to consciousness following a private trance sitting I had with him in May 2000. It is important that you become familiar with his voice. It is important that you appreciate his personality so that you can compare this with the various Spirit people who make use of his physical body. I would remind you that whilst he is in that state of deep trance, he is totally unaware of all that takes place through and around him. To all intents and purposes he is in a state of deep sleep.

Recording - Track 1 (40seconds). Transcript p.72

Section 2 — Séance - 8th July 1999.
White Feather.

The voice you are now going to hear is from Stewart's vocal cords, but White Feather has taken over Stewart's brain and body. White Feather is his Spirit guide and always opens a public séance with his protection and love.

Recording - Track 2 (2min.02seconds). Transcript p.72

Section 3 — Séance - 8th July 1999.
Christopher.

In this section you hear Christopher, a child in Spirit, who plays an important role in relaxing people. This usually takes place at the beginning of a public séance. It is very important to have a relaxed atmosphere otherwise the Spirit people will not be able to come through. Notice the difference in personalities and remember that it is Stewart's body that is being borrowed all the time.

Recording - Track 3 (1min..33seconds). Transcript p.73

Section 4   - Séance - 8th July 1999.
Freda.

Stewart's mind is still disconnected from his brain as Freda takes her turn in controlling the human instrument. Freda is a lady in Spirit who is now using the medium's vocal cords, this is why she sounds more like a man and you will hear her explaining the reason why she does so and how limiting she finds it.

Recording - Track 4 (2min.13seconds). Transcript p.74

Section 5   - Séance - 8th July 1999.
Walter Stinson.

We now have Walter, a Canadian who died in 1911. He is a lovely gentleman and is very charming (particularly to the ladies). Walter is the Spirit team member responsible for generating all the manifesting physical phenomena. Before this can be successfully achieved, he must first withdraw from the medium the vital, living, dynamic energy known to Spiritualists as Ectoplasm. This energy/substance is the very foundation upon which all physical phenomena rest and depend and upon which it is created and demonstrated.

Recording - Track 5 (2min.40seconds). Transcript p.75

General Comment

You have now listened to four different Spirit people all using

Stewart's body in turn. These Spirit people are the Spirit team and have been using Stewart's body as an instrument for some time; this is why they are so eloquent when speaking through his vocal cords. When you sit with a medium in trance, you do not have to sit in the dark. I have seen Stewart in trance in the red light and his eyes have been shut all the time. When a Spirit person leaves his body, he slumps back into the chair like a rag doll and remains in that position until another Spirit person animates the body. When he comes out of trance, he is unaware of what has been happening. Stewart is giving very precious service to the Spirit people by allowing them to use his brain and body, making it possible for them to communicate with us. The regular Spirit team - White Feather, Christopher, Freda and Walter are always at hand to protect him, although trance is not as dangerous to a medium as the production of physical phenomena.

Section 6   Private sitting - 25th May 2000.
Katie's father speaks.

Our loved ones in Spirit also get a chance to try and use Stewart in trance. My father, who died in 1991, came through to talk to me. It was difficult for him to use the medium, although he did extremely well considering he did not have the same experience as the regular Spirit team. You can hear what problems he had when he spoke for the first time.
Recording - Track 6 (1min.21seconds). Transcript p.76

Section 7   - Séance - 31st August 2000.
Independent voice.

When Dad spoke through Stewart in trance, it didn't sound like my father, simply because he was using the medium's brain and vocal cords. The Spirit people are developing Direct Voice so hopefully, in time, Dad will be able to talk to me using his own voice, directly from his own mind, expressing his own personality without any interference from the medium.

To do this a Spirit person speaks through an ectoplasmic replica of the human voice box. Here we have a Spirit person experimenting with the independent, or Direct Voice.
Recording - Track 7 (2min.38seconds). Transcript p.77

General Comment

When the Spirit people speak directly to us, independent of the medium they often do so by means of a séance room 'trumpet'. Initially the voice is created within an ectoplasmic voice box which is a temporary mechanism created by the Spirit world. The voice then passes through an ectoplasmic tube, one end of which is connected to this voice box and the other end to the trumpet, which acts as a megaphone, amplifying the voice to make it audible to us. Stewart has two of these trumpets in the séance room, they are simple funnel shaped objects made out of lightweight material and are about 18"(45cm) in length with a 4"(10cm) diameter at the large end, tapering down to 1"(2.5cm) diameter at the small end. We are able to see them in the dark because they have luminous paint around the broader ends. The trumpets gyrate and dance around from sitter to sitter, sometimes shooting straight up to the ceiling and swiftly down to the floor. One trumpet will pause directly in front of a sitter and, perhaps, tap a shoulder, stroke an arm or come to rest on a lap. There is a lot of movement in the total darkness and any fraudulent activity would be an impossibility, for the trumpets never hit, collide with or crash into any of the sitters, or any object in the room.

Section 8   - Séance - 8th July 1999.
Walter materialises hand.

Ectoplasm is also used for materialisation. Walter used this to form his own hand from the ectoplasm that emanated from Stewart on to a table. All this was done in the red light and I actually saw Walter's hand develop from a living, rolling mist and paste-like substance. His hand was warm to the touch as he placed it on mine. Listen to our words when we saw the ectoplasm flow on to the table.

Recording - Track 8 (4min.22seconds). Transcript p.78

Section 9 - Séance - 25th May 2000.
Materialised Form.

When the energy has reached its peak our Spirit friends can then fully materialise; by this I mean that they can actually walk among us in the darkness of the séance room. We can hear them and they are for a short time solid to the touch. Through the miracle of ectoplasm, they have once again taken on physical form. Here, a Spirit person is actually speaking from his own materialised body.

Recording - Track 9 (3min.30seconds). Transcript p.80

Section 10 - Séance - 4th May 2000.
Walter and matter through matter.

In this section, Walter demonstrates how living matter can pass through solid matter. Stewart's wrists are fastened to the chair arms with tough plastic straps, these automatically lock themselves in position and are impossible to break. The only way that he can free himself is to ask a circle member to cut him free with wire cutters. What you are going to hear on the recording, is how the Spirit people freed Stewart's arm by dematerialising the plastic strap whilst his hands were firmly held by the sitters at both sides of him. When Stewart's arm was free in the air, a circle member tugged hard at the strap to find it was still intact round the chair arm and it was definitely not broken.

Recording - Track 10 (2min.54seconds). Transcript p.82

General Comment

A self-illuminated light growing from a pinprick to the size of a snowball; Spirit writing on paper; drumsticks banging on the table; ectoplasmic rods touching our fingers; water sprinkling on some sitters , these only a few of the psychic phenomena we experienced.

Section 11   - Private sitting - 25th May 2000.
Freda explains ectoplasm.

'What is ectoplasm made of?' This is a popular question and one which I put to Freda at a private sitting which I attended on 25 May 2000. She emphasised the danger of ectoplasm as she explained this rare phenomenon as best as she could.
Recording - Track 11 (7min.58seconds). Transcript p.83

Section 12   - Séance - 25th May 2000.
Walter demonstrates ectoplasm in the light.

The promise, which was made in Section 11, was fulfilled at a later séance, held on the same day. Walter let us all see the ectoplasm come from Stewart's mouth. We cannot show you what it looked like, but you may like to listen to our delight when we saw it all happen.
Recording - Track 12 (3min.38seconds). Transcript p.86

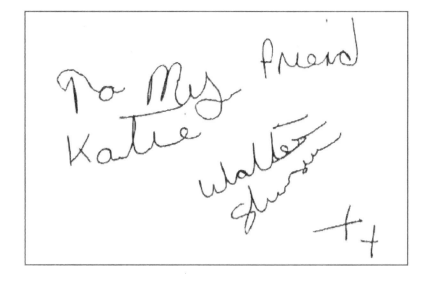

Section 13 - Séance - 31st August 2000.
Walter writes.

In the red light, I watched the ectoplasm form into two pincers on top of a table and pick up a pen. In front of everyone's eyes, this ectoplasmic form wrote a message on a piece of paper, which is shown on the previous page.
Recording - Track 13 (2min.12seconds). Transcript p.88

General Comment

This book and CD only explain what can happen and is happening. It does not emphasise the unconditional love and important messages our Spirit friends have transmitted and expressed to the circle collectively and to individual sitters. When it comes to personal evidence, however, only the individual concerned can guarantee its authenticity.

Section 14 - Séance - 4th May 2000.
Walter giving evidence to Katie and Christine.

A loved one in Spirit often connects with your thought energy, especially when you are feeling happy and the atmosphere is in complete harmony. My sister, Christine, often thought of Mum when she did the ironing. (When Mum was alive on the Earth plane, she was very particular about her ironing). Christine now resides in a narrow boat and living in such conditions, the ironing is never done as Mum would have liked it. Christine often wondered what Mum would think of this. Listen to Walter transmitting Mum's thoughts about the subject of ironing to us. I didn't know what Walter was talking about until Christine told me after the séance. This evidence tells us how our loved ones in Spirit are much closer to us than we think.
Recording - Track 14 (1min.39seconds). Transcript p.90

Section 15 - Séance - 31st August 2000.
Christopher.

We have not heard Christopher since Section 3, so let's bring him back in. You will hear Christopher's chirpy voice at the beginning of a séance announcing that a Ronald Hill is here, (and he can't spell!).

Recording - Track 15 (53seconds). Transcript p.90

Section 16 - Séance - 31st August 2000.
Freda helping a communicator.

Later in that same séance, after Freda's introduction, I had a conversation with the above mentioned Ronald. Ronald was the first husband of my friend Georgina Brake (*see p.30*). He was killed in action during the Second World War. After she had received Ronald's blessing, when he materialised at a Helen Duncan séance in 1941, Ena married Bob. Ena's health was deteriorating and Ronald was concerned for his wife. This conversation took place on 31 August 2000; it was my last visit to the séance room in Hull before Ena passed to the higher life on 5 February 2001. Ronald knew what was going to happen and got this message through while he could. Chiefy is Ena's Spirit friend.

You will also hear Mum trying to talk to me, but as it was very difficult for her to control the medium, Freda stepped in to help her get her message across.

Recording - Track 16 (7min.49seconds). Transcript p.91

Section 17 - Séance - November 2000.
Freda gives evidence.

In this section we invite you to listen to Freda, (through Stewart in trance), transmitting thought waves from the Spirit World at Stewart's penultimate public demonstration with over 80 people in attendance. This was held in

November 2000 at a Spiritualist church in the South of England, where Stewart was a total stranger to everyone other than his immediate team. Although the séance that night was almost two hours long and included physical phenomena, we have selected, (with the recipient's permission), an extract of evidential communication.

Recording - Track 17 (14min.40seconds). Transcript p.94

Section 18   - Private sitting - 25th May 2000.
Freda speaks about acceptance of the 'Truth'.

In the modern world of today so much can be done to prove the reality of that world which awaits us all beyond the grave. However, no amount or quality of communicated evidence will appeal to the closed mind. This work is for the open-minded who will carefully consider the facts presented. At this point let me assure you that I am aware (as is the Spirit World) that there are conscious and unconscious mediumistic frauds just as there are frauds in most professions. Conscious frauds in terms of mediumship are those who purposely set out to deceive for monetary gain. Unconscious frauds are pseudo mediums whose gifts, rather than being genuine, owe everything to an over-active imagination. They are, in fact, people who unknowingly deceive themselves into believing that they are what they are not. Listen to what Freda has to say about this.

Recording - Track 18 (4min.30seconds). Transcript p.101

Section 19   - Private sitting - 25th May 2000.
Walter talks to Katie.

The Spirit people are only human beings who have gone before us and they are concerned about our ignorance of the truth. This is what Walter said to me.

Recording - Track 19 (4min.10seconds). Transcript p.102

Section 20 - Séance - 8th July 1999.
The Spirit Team says 'Goodnight' - July 8th 1999.

I thought it would be appropriate to use the final section by inviting you to listen to our Spirit team expressing their good wishes to the circle members at the end of a séance held on 8 July 1999.

Recording - Track 20 (2min.56seconds). Transcript p.104

I hope that this information and the accompanying CD have helped to pave the way to a better understanding of life and reality beyond death. It has been my hope, purpose and desire to remove the needless fear of death.

Of course there are, and always will be, many questions to ask, but what is most important is the free flow of the Spirit. Therefore, whatever I choose to plan ahead may not always be. It is for our Spirit friends to decide what is possible.

Part Two is well on its way and will include interesting and more advanced evidence on Direct Voice, Materialisation and self-luminous Spirit lights. I intend to carry on with my work as long as our Spirit friends wish me to do so.

It is my sincere hope that this series of books and the accompanying CDs will help our Spirit friends to remove doubt and confusion in the minds of so many people upon this Earth concerning mankind's eternal destiny.

Reports from America,
Switzerland & England

Our Spirit friends are continuously sending out their loving thoughts, ever caring, ever patient; ever hopeful in helping us to break the barriers that we set upon ourselves.

It doesn't matter which country you live in, or how far from home you may be, the thought contact is unchanged.

The Transatlantic Séance Experiment

This fascinating experiment took place when direct contact was made by our Spirit friends from the séance room in Kingston-upon-Hull in Northern England to Oswego in New York State, North America. These two places, so far apart in the material world, were joined together in one thought space - and this is not telepathy! - the book test adequately illustrates this.

For over thirty years Stewart made an exhaustive study of Spiritualism's history - particularly that relating to physical mediumship. During the late 1980's he made contact with Noel Riley Heagerty who lives in Oswego in the state of New York, America, and like Stewart had spent many years similarly researching the whole subject.

This mutual interest was to result in many years' lively

correspondence. However, in consequence of what is to follow, it is important that readers should understand that what passed between them was principally in respect of their research. Very little of a personal nature ever arose.

In the Autumn of 1994, Riley Heagerty was to suggest what later became known as the 'Transatlantic Experiment'. He wanted to ascertain whether Stewart's Spirit controls could possibly lock in to his own vibration, and in order to assist, he sent over to England a lock of his hair and also a small photograph of himself. Stewart's Circle - although never having previously attempted such an ambitious experiment, agreed to try, and wrote back sending a copy of their own séance music. Their Spirit controls asked that Riley Heagerty should sit at exactly the same time as the Circle over in England and play the séance music cassette throughout.

On 1st November 1994, the attempt was made with Mr. Heagerty sitting at his home in Oswego, USA, and the Circle in their regular séance room in England. Within minutes of the commencement of the séance, Stewart was controlled by his regular Spirit guides and it quickly became clear that the entire proceedings would be concentrated upon this unique experiment. The séance was recorded on cassette tape and a copy of it was despatched to America the following day for Mr. Heagerty's analysis.

Two weeks later Stewart and the Circle were to receive a detailed report from him and the following March an account of this highly successful experiment was to be published by two Spiritualist journals. What follows is Mr. Riley Heagerty's report in brief, which I have decided to include in this publication since, in my opinion, it illustrates forcefully the fact that distance is no object to the Spirit people.

I also feel that this experiment goes a long way towards establishing the independence, from the medium, of the

52

manifesting personalities, Walter Stinson and little Christopher. I am satisfied that both demonstrated their own individual intelligence, and I take the view that for posterity and for the great truth of 'Survival' the details of this experiment must be recorded and preserved.

'The Noel Riley Heagerty Report'

Introduction

Stewart's circle arranged the séance procedure. I sat at 3 o'clock (American Time) in the afternoon, in dim red light, and played the exact musical tape which the circle played as they sat at 8 o'clock (English Time). I then concentrated my thoughts and vibrations upon Walter Stinson, White Feather and young Christopher. That is all I did. I had absolutely no idea, until I received the tape of their sitting that Walter and Christopher actually came to my house.

Stewart and I never once mentioned to each other that the Spirits would be coming to America. I had more or less expected them to simply take a "reading" from the lock of hair and the tiny picture. I was absolutely stunned, wondrously so, when I heard the tape; absolutely shocked. There has never been a Spiritualist in my sitting room, ever, and I have never described my room to any person on this Earth, nor my house, or any of its contents or structure. I have known Stewart for some years. Our interests are in research and physical mediumship. We have shared very little on a personal level outside of our obvious love of physical mediumship.

The Report

First, I must say what a tremendous, mature and powerful circle you have; one shining light in the firmament of reality. Now, let me first tell you that, yes indeed, I was sitting right at the exact time as all of you were, right to the minute. I had the international operator give me the exact time and I set my clock accordingly. My thoughts were centred on your circle, your energy and your Spirit controls especially. I visualised a white beam of light going from here to there. I had the exact music playing and soft, dim red light throughout.

<u>Core Specifics</u>

Let us now consider Walter and some of the hard core specifics of the experiment. Although I was intending to wait until the end of this report before commenting upon the accuracy of the experiment, I have decided not to do so. Brace yourselves - I would score it almost a clear and complete 100% success. As I listen to the recording once again I shall translate it and record my comments.

'A large house' - *correct. I live in a very large, pre-civil War house, built in 1847.*

'Five steps up to the front door' - *correct.* 'A very large door' - *absolutely correct.*

'In the door, right there, are the stairs' - *correct.*

'Up the stairs we go, a railing' - *correct.*

Natural wood' - *explicitly correct; the rail and the stairs are pure mahogany.*

'Stairs turn' - *correct.*

'They then continue to go up' - *correct.*

'Home of peace' - *absolutely correct in all regards.*

'We now go along a long corridor, and there are rooms on each side' - *both of which are correct.*

'At the end of the corridor there is a room' - *correct.*

'Walking up to the top of the house' - *absolutely correct. I live in the attic of the house.*

'The richness of the room; several pictures on the wall; a room that is filled with the power of the Spirit' - *nothing could be more correct than these statements about this room.*

'Opposite the door, to the right, a desk' - *perfectly correct.*

Above it are bookshelves' - *correct.*

'To the right, as with the shelf above the desk, is a bookshelf - all being filled with books' - *correct again.*

'A burial ground not far from the house' - *correct.*

'Opposite the door to the left, a window which is covered over' - *this is astonishingly correct.*

'The gentleman sits without shoes' - *correct. (For the experiment absolutely no shoes were worn).*

'An irritation in the right arm.' - *On the very day of the experiment I was in our back yard trying to get our snow-blower working. I replaced a spark plug and pulled the rope to start the machine up. With full force my right elbow hit a stack of firewood directly behind me. I thought that I had broken it. As I type this report, (15th November) it still hurts and when I sat for the experiment my elbow was extremely painful.*

'A strange smell in the room' - *correct - the room has a continuous cranberry candle aroma.*

Let me now move on to Christopher's input.

'A big bookcase, lots and lots of books' - *perfectly correct, of course.*

'Third shelf down, 14th book in from the left - a pamphlet and next to this is a book with a torn cover' - *The pamphlet is of all things* - Visits by Our Friends from the Other Side - *written of course, by Tom Harrison and there is a book with a torn cover next to it.*

(Readers will be interested to hear that the author Tom Harrison should have been sitting with the Circle on the night of the experiment but at the last moment was unable to attend).

Most incredibly, Christopher refers to a drawing of a ship, (A sailing ship - he says) - *and there is a beautiful painting right above my old leather chair of a group of sailboats. If you were to stand back, or better still, stand back and refer to it as a child would, it looks like one ship.*

'Dogs barking' - *they are barking all the time over here. There is no doubt in my mind that during the experiment a dog was barking. The four houses that surround my house all have dogs!*

'The slight step up into the room' - *This has got to be the floor right in front of my door. Because of the chimney the floor goes up like a hill, and then down again. Amazing indeed.*

This completes my report. The sailboats, the cemetery, the covered window, the bookcases, the Harrison pamphlet, no shoes, the internal details of the house. There is absolutely no getting around the accuracy of this 'Transatlantic Experiment'.

I would like to thank Noel Riley Heagerty for his permission to print this very interesting report - and we now leave America to go -

Over to Switzerland

In May 1999, Stewart, together with Circle leaders Ray and June Lister, visited Switzerland, where he delivered three lectures on physical phenomena with each being followed by

56

an experimental séance. The arrangements for the visit had been made by Dr. Hans U. Schaer of Zurich, whom Stewart had met some years earlier at a seminar on physical mediumship held on the South Coast of England. Dr. Schaer, had liased with both the 'Parapsychological Association of Zurich' and the 'PSI Association - Basle' (Basler PSI Verein) who hosted these special events. Whilst in Switzerland, Stewart gave two lectures and demonstrations in Zurich and one in Basle, with some members of the Associations flying in from all over the world, in order to attend. On each occasion between 80 and 100 people were present. What made these lectures and séances unique, was the fact that for the very first time they were conducted outside of England.

Additionally, they had to be translated by an interpreter as many who attended were unable to understand English. Literally, up until the commencement of the first séance, no one knew if the Spirit communicators would be able to work in such a way; whether, in fact, the presence of the interpreter would have an adverse effect upon the proceedings. However, as things turned out, all fears and concerns proved to be groundless and, in many ways, the séances were somewhat enhanced.

The whole trip proved to be quite a success and, as a result, a great many people were able to personally witness and experience the coming together of the two worlds in a physical manner.

The following August, an extensive report of Stewart's work appeared in 'Para' (A Swiss journal for Parapsychology and Esotericism) which is published by the 'PSI Association - Basle'. Under the main title of 'Spirit Hands, Dematerialised Bands and Flying Trumpets' its Chairman Lucius Werthmuller gave a fair and impartial report concerning the principal aspects of the séances which he had personally attended. His Association was founded in 1967 and has several thousand members worldwide. It is one of the patrons of the annual 'Basle PSI conference' - Europe's largest congress on the border areas of science.

What follows is an abbreviated version of his article. Whilst remaining faithful and true to the original, I have selected extracts which have particular relevance to this publication and which should prove to be of particular interest to readers.

<u>Spirit Hands, Dematerialised Bands and FlyingTrumpets</u>

Experimental Séances with Stewart Alexander and his Home Circle

By: Lucius Werthmuller. (Edited by Katie Halliwell).

<u>Stewart Alexander in Switzerland</u>

In the middle of May, Stewart Alexander and members of his Home Circle held three experimental séances in Switzerland; the first ones outside of Great Britain. I had the opportunity to take part at two of these. During the first part of the evening Stewart spoke about the history of Spiritualism and also about the different forms of mediumistic manifestations. He then went on to describe his own development and told how things started to happen at his own Circle. Finally, he and Dr. Hans Schaer told us about the order of events for the séance which would follow and gave instructions as to how we must conduct ourselves - what we could and could not do at the séance.

After a break, during which people were asked to leave the room so that everything could be prepared, the participants were asked to return one by one. Everyone was checked because no matches, lighters, flash cameras, or illuminated

58

watches were permitted in the room. The reason for this safety check was due to the fragile state of the body of the medium during the séance. A sudden interruption during the meeting by a light of any kind, (the séance took place in a completely darkened room) could cause serious damage to the health of the medium.

Stewart Alexander prepared himself in another room and already seemed to be far away when he was led into the room. He took his place in an armchair (Plain wood - no upholstery) and was tied to his seat. Both of his arms were tied to the wooden chair arms with a special plastic ribbon, that later had to be cut off with strong wire cutters. All these events were controlled by a participant.

The Séance Starts

At the two sessions that I attended, the first Spirit being who said hello, was White Feather. Following some words of welcome a being, calling himself Christopher, came next and explained that he had left the Earth at the age of six-and-a-half years. His purpose is to lighten the mood, which is sometimes a little tense at the beginning of such a séance. Full of humour, he cheers everyone up in a child-like and lovable way. The changes in the voice of the medium, from a deep voice to a childish high voice, were amazing.

The third Spirit visitor was Freda Johnson who spoke about the Spirit World and its connection to ours. It was she who went on to give evidential messages to some of the participants.

The fourth who spoke was Walter Stinson who is mainly responsible for the physical phenomena which develops at Stewart's séances. Walter, who died when he was a young man, was the brother of the renowned Physical Medium 'Margery', whose mediumship, back in the 1920's and 1930's had been the subject of much controversy. In the many reports of her séances, Walter appeared as her principal Spirit control. Now, he says, he would like to finish the work he initially commenced through his sister's mediumship.

The Physical Phenomena

The first experiment performed involved the medium's arms being freed from the unbreakable plastic bonds that secured them to the wooden arms of the chair. Then, without human intervention, he was tied again to his armchair. (see the interview with Tina Luscher). Then, a lady was asked to sit at a small table facing the medium and to place one of her hands on the glass table top. For this experiment a red light bulb was turned on, which was fixed under the glass surface.

A cloud of ectoplasm was then seen, out of which after some seconds, the shape of a hand appeared. This materialised structure took the hand of the lady and turned it over whilst slapping it and this was heard by everyone. Then several participants said that they also were being touched by a hand. (This phenomena only happened at the séance in Zurich that I attended - see the interviews with Gabriella von Glasow and Ruth Hess).

At both the séances I participated in, 'flying trumpets' - cones of lightweight aluminium marked with fluorescent colour - rose in the air and flew through the room. First they knocked on the floor; then they rose hesitantly. Later, they flew with high speed throughout the whole room. In Zurich, where the séance room was around six metres high, they rose to the ceiling, knocked on the walls and completed the most exciting flight manoeuvres at breathtaking speed. They also touched several participants.

At the séance in Basle they also flew for a while, but on that occasion they remained in the front part of the room. I

60

myself was touched twice in a very gentle way by a flying trumpet. Several times the sitters were asked by the trance communicators to sing a song, in order - as they said - to 'raise the atmosphere'. At both the séances Christopher tapped out the rhythm of the songs with drumsticks on the table.

An additional phenomenon occurred at the séance in Basle. At one point in the proceedings a faint voice called out to a participant by name. However, it was so soft that it could not be heard throughout the whole room.

Just before the séance ended, Walter asked if anyone understood the number 184 and the name Elsa, or something similar. It was my wife who recognised that the name of a road was meant, and that the number was relevant. Indeed, we work at the Elsasserstrasse... Unfortunately, we didn't get a message because Walter told us that he had to conclude the séance because the great heat (The temperature in the room) was beginning to affect the health of the medium and therefore have a detrimental effect upon communication.

A point of interest is that during the séance Stewart twice came out of the trance state due to the heat in the room, yet strangely the phenomena continued. The trumpets were still flying and a Direct Voice could be heard speaking.

When we switched on the light at the end of the Basle séance, there was another surprise awaiting us. The shirt that Stewart had been wearing underneath his pullover at the beginning of the séance was now seen to be lying on a small table at a distance of one metre from the medium. This happened in spite of the fact that his arms were still fixed with plastic bands to the chair arms and had to be cut with wire cutters in order to release him. It seems that his shirt had been dematerialised - that it had passed through his body and through his pullover, and then materialised again.

After a short break Stewart was available for questions.

The séances I attended impressed me deeply but, to be fair, it must be said that the arrangements under which they were conducted left room for speculation by sceptical people. But for me personally, I am absolutely convinced that I witnessed genuine paranormal phenomena. The sincere and modest behaviour of Stewart Alexander and his fellow members convinced me even more.

Additional Reports

Tina Luscher

The trance personality, Walter Stinson, asked me to sit at the side of Stewart Alexander and, to grasp his tied-down right hand - this I did with my left. I then reached out with my right hand and felt the special plastic band, which was tight around his arm and the arm of the chair. Suddenly there was a jerk and together our arms shot up into the air and remained there for about two minutes. During this time I felt the armrest and realised that the band had disappeared. Then, there was another jerk and our arms went down and I again felt the medium's arm and realised that again his arm was fixed tightly with a plastic ribbon.

After the séance, we discovered that it had been tied with the plastic band that had lain in reserve on the small table, prior to the séance commencing. After this experiment I was suddenly seized by a hand. It was obvious to me that this could not have been the hand of anyone present in the room. I was certain that it was a materialised hand. In one respect this was a shock to me, but it also touched me deeply because some weeks earlier I had really wished for a substantial contact with the Spirit World. I had to smile inside after the initial shock, and was really very happy about this solid touch, and particularly since I had participated at this séance without any expectations.

Gabriella von Glasow

During the séance I realised that we have to communicate with the Spirit World in order to maintain a strong connection. (*How perfectly true. KH*). As the flying trumpets came to me, I talked with Christopher who was speaking through the Medium and I was then touched gently on the nose and then on the cheek by the trumpets. Shortly afterwards Walter announced himself back by inquiring who the lady was who had just flirted with Christopher? He wanted to know my name, and he then invited me to sit at his table facing Stewart. I accepted, and once I was seated he asked me to report clearly to all present everything that I could see and feel. I placed my hand, with palm uppermost, on the glass tabletop, which was illuminated from beneath by a red light. Soon a dark mass appeared at the edge of the table, out of which fingers and then a hand slowly formed. A warm soft and pleasant hand of a man grasped my hand. It was not bony, but fleshy, and it caressed my hand and finally left with a firm handshake. The hand then dissolved and again became a black mass. Walter said to me: "I hope that you had as much pleasure as I had" and, I replied, "I sure did". I was very touched. This contact made me very happy. It was the first time that I had experienced such a physical contact.

Ruth Hess

Freda addressed me and said that a lady was with her who has the same name as I have. I asked if the second name was Christen, which she affirmed. Ruth Christen is a very dear friend who died in 1982 of a brain tumour. We had been close friends and I had accompanied her on her last journey. I feel her presence, so the communication made sense to me. She told me how happy she was to have the opportunity to be in contact this way and, was sorry that it had taken such a long time. She also told me that in the Spirit World she takes part in a group similar to the one I lead on Earth. She confirmed that this Spiritual work is very important and that I really should go on with it. In fact, at home we do have a meditation Circle.

Then, I was asked to approach the table and to place a hand on it. A rubbery mass appeared at the opposite end and gradually formed itself into fingers and then into a hand and then it became alive. It then laid itself upon mine, turned my hand on its side and then audibly pressed, and tapped it. I had had a similar experience once before and therefore it was clear to me that there is a Spirit World and I took this as a further confirmation.

The above reports were edited from a translation copy of the 'Para' article.

I would like to thank Lucius Werthmuller for his introductory report and his permission for me to edit the translated version of the 'Para' article.

We now return to England to read a report from Psychic News who kindly granted us permission to print one of their articles which was published in December 2000.

Music - Trumpets & White Feather

The members and friends of Redland Spiritualist Church had the privilege of welcoming medium Stewart Alexander to Bristol on the 9th and 10th of October. On the Monday evening, Stewart and twenty-five guests sat for a private materialisation circle at the home of Doug Powell. This proved to be a wonderful experience for all present, and what follows is a brief description of what took place. Stewart was securely bound to his chair at the ankles, wrists and waist with heavy-duty cord. (this, of course, is to exclude any possibility of fraud). All circle members were then frisked for any items which should not be brought into the room, like cameras, torches, matches, etc. Any light from these items could cause serious damage to a materialisation medium and Stewart is always well protected by June and Ray Lister, his minders, organisers and circle members. His safety is of paramount importance to them and their devotion to Stewart is plainly evident. Jenny Pike, Vice-President of the Church, then opened with a brief prayer and taped music was played by June.

It was only a question of minutes before Stewart's 'doorkeeper' White Feather began to speak in his distinctive Native American accent. He welcomed all present and expressed his joy at the opportunity to build a bridge of communication between the two worlds. He congratulated Doug on ensuring that the conditions of the room were excellent for the purpose of the Circle, (i.e. fully blacked out with no possibility of intrusive light). White Feather then 'popped out' (in his words!) and a few moments later, Christopher 'popped in.' Everyone was delighted to hear the voice of a small child and the atmosphere was charged with energy from so much laughter as Christopher proceeded to charm the sitters with his light hearted humour. He assured everyone that he was going to be very "respectable," as he had been told there were a lot of spiritual people in the room, so he was going to watch his "Qs and his Ps" and not say anything naughty! However, one or two naughty things were said despite his promise! He told Jenny that he was in love with her and then had a 'banter' with Doug, asking him if he had hit his thumb with a hammer. (Doug, in fact, had a plaster in his thumb which could not have been visible in the pitch darkness).

Christopher assured anyone who was nervous that there was no need to be - "If a ghost appeared in the room now, I would be the first one out of the door!"

The next communicator was Walter Stinson, the brother and guide to the well-known Spiritualist pioneer, Marjory Crandon. He wasted no time in telling the sitters that if they expected wise and elevated speeches, they would be disappointed, as the purpose of the sitting was simply to link the two worlds in love and harmony. Again, the atmosphere was lightened by laughter as Walter flirted with the ladies present! He explained that the energy needed from the medium for physical manifestation would take time to generate and could not be rushed. Many, he said, would feel uncomfortable around the solar plexus, as material would be 'borrowed' for the same purpose. He assured everyone that it would be returned later. He then asked if anyone would like to ask a question. A lady responded and was immediately invited to sit beside the medium and hold his hand. There were indeed, many answers to many questions, in what was to follow. She was asked to place her right hand over her left hand and then to gently feel the strap binding Stewart's hand to the chair. She then announced excitedly, that "he had raised his hand up above his head," which she also announced, "was quite impossible!" Walter explained that she had witnessed the phenomenon of matter passing through matter. Permission was given for the lights to be slightly raised and all were astounded to see that Stewart's arm was free of the restraint that was still firmly tied to the chair. Walter explained that this was no miracle but was only a demonstration of natural law and that the important thing was that our two worlds were as one. The lady sitter was again excited to report to the others that a third hand had materialised and had patted her (audibly to everyone) on her arm. She was then invited to remain behind after the circle for a private sitting as there was 'a football team' of loved ones in the Spirit

World, waiting to speak with her.

Music was played next and the energy in the room was heightened. Two trumpets, edged in luminous paint, began to proceed around the room, touching the sitters one by one on the hand, knee or face, floating effortlessly up to the ceiling and around in circles, all this to the sound of 'Ahhh...Oooo...lovely.' as everyone was entranced by the experience. Even the medium was allowed to wake up for a few moments to see the trumpets. Very soon after this, a 'speaking mechanism' was produced from ectoplasm, by the Spirit friends for the purpose of communication. This voice box was detached from the medium and the voice was audible from a different location. This communicator spoke articulately about the wonderful reality of Spirit communication; "When we work together my friends, we become a united team, we become as one. So many Spiritualists in the past and in the present, have been unwilling to share their experience with those who know so little about this truth. Imagine what the outcome would be, if all who were privy to this knowledge would take it out into the world and share it with all who would listen. We cannot do this alone, my friends; we require your help. Your world would truly become a heaven upon earth if only there was a greater knowledge and understanding of life." At this point, the voice box began to fail and became too weak to function and communication was transferred back to the medium.

The next communicator introduced herself as Freda Johnson in a very 'school-marm-ish' voice. All were called to attention to listen to something that Freda wished everyone to understand. "It is often asked," she said, "If Freda Johnson is a lady, why does she so often sound like a gentleman? What you have to remember, dears, is that I am speaking through Stewart; I am using his bits and his pieces and I can tell you, that it is extremely uncomfortable!" Freda then went on to give excellent clairvoyance to several of the sitters. Jenny was given a message from her mother, with many intimate details, which were only known to the two of them. Freda then said that she would allow her mother to attempt to speak directly through the medium, but not to expect her to be as expert at communication as the guides, as it took many years of practice to perfect the technique. A very emotional exchange followed in which Jenny was left in no doubt that her mother had indeed spoken with her (although with great effort and difficulty). Freda then returned and made everyone laugh by saying that Jenny's mother and herself both admired the same film star, Clark Gable. Walter then returned and organised another demonstration of materialisation. This time, it was Jenny's turn to be amazed. Walter extracted sufficient ectoplasm to build a hand, which Jenny recognised unmistakably as her mother's hand. Another hand was then materialised in the centre of the table, which many of the sitters were able to see because of its luminosity. One of the sitters was then invited to come and hold the hand, which she described as firm, warm and very much alive!

Before White Feather's final words of blessing, Walter closed the evening by thanking everyone for supplying the energy through their love and kind thoughts. He apologised that, on this occasion, he was unable to leave the cabinet and walk around the room, but, unfortunately, there was insufficient energy generated to do so. Nevertheless, everyone present was well pleased with the wonderful experience gained and left the room in a buzz of excitement.

The following day, Stewart gave a further demonstration of trance mediumship to a packed Church Guild. Stewart began with a short talk on how his mediumship had developed, explaining that he, Ray and June, had been sitting together in a circle for over thirty years. After the talk,

Stewart left the room to compose himself and then returned and quickly slipped into a trance. Again, White Feather, Walter, Freda and Christopher were in attendance with the same high standard of communication. The Church Secretary and her mother were given the opportunity to speak to their father and husband through the medium. A very emotional exchange followed, which had the whole audience in tears, as indisputable evidence was given, including the name of the gentleman (and the name of his mother-in-law who had accompanied him) and recalled incidents relating to their life together.

Stewart Alexander is a self-effacing, non-egotistical, genuine person, whose warmth and charisma permeate the room. Those in attendance at these two events thank him and his supporters, June and Ray Lister, for sharing their knowledge of the great truth of survival.

This is the end of the Psychic News report. It is nice to hear other people's views. The great truth of survival is indeed an awesome reality and I hope, like me, you have enjoyed reading these reports.

*We recommend that readers should not attempt
to sit in a circle or try to contact
the Spirit people without prior knowledge and
understanding of procedure and the protection
and guidance of an experienced medium..*

Transcript
for
Séance Recordings
Sections 1 to 20

Audiotyped by Ann Harrison

"Being deaf myself, I know only too well how invaluable this transcript will be for readers with hearing difficulties. I would like to express a special thank you to Ann Harrison as this transcript would not have been possible without her generous offer to audio type from the tape recordings.

Readers will also find the transcript useful should they wish to study extracts in detail without having to search for any specific details within the tracks on the CDs."

Katie Halliwell (April 2003)

Part One - Evidence of Survival After Death

Throughout the transcript where there is a brief response from another person into a long continuous passage the brief responses have been put into brackets to keep the flow of the conversation.

And having introduced each speaker by name the first time they speak, the names have then been shortened to an initial where possible.

Section 1 *(Track 1; Intro p40)*
Stewart Alexander.

(Stewart and Katie speak alternately)

Stewart. Right Katie	**Katie.** Ok?
Stewart. Yes, fine	**K.** You Ok?
S. Yes thank you.	**K.** I thank you.
S. No June?..... June's gone?	**K.** Er, Yes
S. Oh God. (sighs)	Katie laughs
S. Oh dear. (Stewart stretches)	**K.** Thank you
S. That's all right Katie	
K. It was a very good experience	
S. Was it OK?	**K.** Yes, yes
S. Lovely. Lovely.	**K.** It was very interesting.
S. Who came? Freda?	**K.** Pardon?
S. Who came?	**K.** Walter and Freda

S. Oh right, right.
K. We had a little scientific discussion.
S. Oh did you.
K. Yes very good, very interesting.
S. Oh did you. Well it's not very often Walter comes you
know, in an afternoon.   **K.** Yes.

(end of section 1)

Section 2 *(Track 2; Intro p40)*
White Feather.

White Feather. White Feather come speak with his brothers
and sisters.
All. Good evening, White Feather/ Welcome
W.F. Once again White Feather is delighted that we have
come together in this place of love.
Ray. Yes, very nice, White Feather.
W.F. Once again, White Feather wants you all to know that

for a short time we shall remove the barrier between our world and yours so that we can come together in love.
All. Thank you, White Feather
W.F. White Feather as always speak very good England.
June. (smiling) Very good, absolutely, yes. Doing well.
(others gently laugh at his joke)
W.F. There is much to be done (**Ray.** That's good.) - and White Feather know that you all bring with you such great love and we return that manyfold.
All. Thank you
W.F. There are many souls in my world who have gathered here tonight all hoping to make contact with you
Various voices. Good / That's nice / Thank you.
W.F. White Feather know that we shall enjoy and share in a wonderful meeting of souls within this room. There is much to be done. White Feather will pop out now.
All. Thank you, White Feather.

(end of Section 2)

Section 3   *(Track 3; Intro p40)*
Christopher.

Christopher. *(shouting)* Katie!   **Katie.** I can hear you.
Chris. Are you sure?   **K.** Yes I can.
Chris. Bloody 'ell, I can't keep this up all night!
(Laughter from everyone)
Ch. *(laughs)* She's lovely isn't she? Yeah. I like you, Katie.
K. I like you too. You're really happy.
Ch. Well I always try to be. 'Ere, Katie if I can explain. When people come to sit with old Stewart, don't tell 'im I called 'im 'old Stewart', (**K.** No I won't) - No. When people come to sit with old Stewart sometimes they are very, very nervous, (**K.** Yes) - so it's my job to relax everybody.
K. Right, and you are doing a good job too.

Ch. Am I?

K. Yes. Yes (*others join in with yeses*)

Ch. Yes, yes, no wonder I like my job. (**K.** That's why.) I'm the best, mate. I've got qualifications in relaxation, (*laughs*) (*and laughter from everyone else*) - Sabine, I've been told I've got to try and speak a little slower, so you can understand. (**Sabine.** Yes I speak German.) - Yes, well I can't speak German. Yes, sometimes people over 'ere say I sound as though I am speaking German! (**June.** Double-dutch!) - Yes, yes but I do my best, Sabine. If you don't understand what I'm talking about, just stop me and I'll repeat it. (**S.** Thank you, thank you) - Yes, yes, it's alright. But don't stop me too often or we'll be here until two in the morning. *(laughter)*

Ch. Heh, hee! I love mi job!

All. We know.

(end of section 3)

Section 4   *(Track 4; Intro p41)*
Freda.

Freda. A wonderful coming together. A wonderful meeting between our two worlds. *(sounds of everyone agreeing.)* - Now I'd like to begin, if I may, by explaining something to those people who've not sat with Stewart before, or rarely sat with Stewart before. May I first of all introduce myself to those souls. My name is Freda Johnson. Now let me say this, that it has been commented upon that my voice... has all the......shall we say, suggests that it is in reality the voice of a male rather than a female but I'm always at pains to point out, forgive me if you have heard me say this before but I do feel that it is important. (**June.** It is important) - What is all important is not the way that I sound but what I have to say. That is all that is important and also of course that I'm able to project, that I'm able to transmit, that I'm able to present my personality, loud and clear to you all. (**June.**- That's important. (*agreement from all.*) - Of course my voice tends to be male-like, simply because I'm speaking through a male organism. I'm surrounded by all this maleness, dears. Ladies here this evening will be interested to hear that it is not very pleasant! (*laughter from all*) - but I have to do the best and work with what I have. (*more laughter from Lucius*) - So this evening I'm delighted to say that I'm quite content with the control, with the quality of control, that I have upon the medium.

Man's voice. You're doing very well.

(end of section 4)

Section 5   *(Track 5; Intro p41)*
Walter Stinson.

Walter. OK, Folks   **All.** OK, Walter

W. You can all hear my voice?   **All.** Yes, Walter.

W. In that case I begin as always by saying - Good evening folks.

All. Good evening Walter. / Welcome

W. What a truly wonderful response as always.

All. Thank you Walter/OK Walter

W. It is a wonderful delight to see you all here this evening.

All. We enjoy it tremendously.

W. Folks, we know that many of you have travelled a great distance to be here. (**Man's voice.** We have indeed.) We know. But we are so delighted (**Man.** Oh, good.) - that you have all joined together. (**Voices.** Yes, yes) - Our purpose in returning, our sole purpose in communicating with your world in this manner is not so folks can witness those things which people in ignorance within your world would consider to be miracles. Hmm? It is not that, folks. It is simply to show you what we can achieve, what we can do, how we can reach out to you all when we have love and harmony. From that, we hope that each of you will leave this room and have confirmed within your mind that man truly is eternal. That communication between our two worlds is a wonderous reality, folks. (**All.** Yes) - People say - but why party tricks, why move illuminated trumpets, why do this and why do that - Hmm? but it is only to show you - it is no party trick; it is only to show you the reality of our world; it is to show you the reality of ourselves; to show you that man is eternal; that our world for a short time can join with yours; that we can come together as one; that is the sole purpose of our return, folks. (**All.** Yes, yes)

(end of section 5)

Section 6   *(Track 6; Intro p42)*
Katie's father speaks.

K's. Father. Ohh! Yes. Kate!
Katie. Come on Dad you're doing very well -
K's. Father. Kate, is that you?   **Katie.** It is indeed.
Father. Oh, I say this is so wonderful.
K. It's nice to talk to you again.
Father. I don't know if you can hear everything I'm trying to say. (**K.** I can yes) - It's rather like trying to speak to you through a fog. (**K.** Yes) - I know that I'm doing what I was told to do but at the same time my mind, I find, is so confused. Oh …. Kate! (**K.** You're doing very well I can hear you very well) - oh… mother's here, we're both together, we're both together……but…I…..oh   (**K.** Keep trying.) - I'm trying so very hard   (**K.** It must be very difficult.) - Oh I can't begin to tell you how difficult this is…..Give our love to them all….give our love to them all….   (**K.** Yes, I will.)

(end of section 6)

Section 7
Independent voice.   *(Track 7; Intro p42)*

June. You'll get there.

Ray. We'll let you know how you are doing

Katie. Is this independent voice?

R. It sounds like it Katie.

J. Come on, that's it

R. I can hear the breath now my friend, I can hear your breath. Yes this is good, this is. Yes that's right. I can hear the volume now, yes, that's it, keep going.

J. Keep going, friend.

R. Once we've got the volume, then we get the clarity of the words, my friend come on.

Voice. I do hope that my......(*more indistinguishable words are heard*)

J. It is getting there. / **R.** we can hear your voice and it is getting clearer. / **J.** It is, it's nice.

Voice. .... difficult to speak.

R. I didn't quite catch that, my friend.

Gaynor. He's endeavouring to speak . It's right next to my cheek. It's right near to me.

Voice. ...speaking mechanism, as always, is so unstable...

G. Yes, the speaking mechanism......

V. *(louder)*...I do hope that you are all able to hear my voice.

G./R. Yes, You are getting clearer now, my friend, yes.

V. I must say that in a sense I find this to be most frustrating.

R. Oh yes, you must do. / **J.** You must do, friend.

G. You're doing well, very well.

R. But you do get better each week, you know that.

V. Well it is very generous of you to say that.

Circle. Well you do /you do, you do./ Really do./It's true.

V. I often feel that perhaps...well it would make the process just a little simpler if I were...if I were able to hear my own voice. (**Ray.** Yes, of course, yes) - It is the fact that I'm unable to do so which I suppose contributes largely to the fact that I'm never quite certain if I'm meeting with any particular level of success.

Circle. Yes. You are, you are doing very well.

V. You can all hear? (**R.** Yes) - Then my friends I would like to say this (**R.** Yes) - that although I am quite aware and conscious of the fact, I'm aware of the fact, that so many who come here would expect that a visitor from my world able to speak in his own voice and in this way to transmit his own thoughts without the burden of the interference, no matter how small, of........

(end of section 7)

Section 8   *(Track 8; Intro p43)*
Walter materialises hand.

Walter. You folks who are sitting a long way from the table, if you wish to stand you may.

Man's voice. Ok. Thank you, thank you, Walter.

Walter. Katie, ma'am.

Ray. (Just so you can see what is going on, that's all)

W. All you folks here I tell you what I hope to be able to do.

R. Ok, Walter / **K.** Thank you.

W. In a moment I shall produce the energy you have heard referred to as ectoplasm. (**K.** Yes I have) - This I hope to be able to show you upon the table top and from that energy I hope to be able to create, to mould, my own hand, folks, but you must tell me if I am meeting with success for I depend and rely upon you. Ok, Ok. Raymondo, may we have the music very quietly.

Ray. Yes, yes, yes.

Music plays. Circle hums along with it.

June. Can you see something coming across the table? Can you Katie?

Ray. Something moving, yes.

J. Something coming across the table top.

R. It's just sort of spreading. Some of it is spreading; some of it is see-through isn't it? **Others.** Yeah, yeah, there is.

R. There's like fingers coming out of it 1,2,3,4. I can see 4, well done friends.

Katie. Fantastic.

Ray. You can see where it is transparent in places. Well done, Walter.

June. Well done, Walter. That was successful Walter.

W. Ok, Ok. (**J.** That was successful Walter.) - You could see? Then Katie ma'am you must do something for me. Can you hear my voice ma'am?

Ray. Katie can you hear him? **Katie.** Yes I can.

W. Ma'am, I would like you to place your right hand upon the table with your palm downwards. That is fine ma'am. I ask you to keep your hand perfectly still. Hmm?

K. Right.

W. I want you to tell the folks exactly what you can feel. Hmm? **Katie.**Yes.

R. What you can see, what you can feel. **K.** Right.

June. Just keep your hand perfectly still, Katie.

R. What it's like warm: cold, hot, anything and everything about it, just keep your hand perfectly still. **K.** Yes.

R. Now there's the lump, shall we say, coming forward, on to the table, reaching towards Katie's hand.

K. It's nearly there but not quite.

R. But the hand hasn't formed yet.

K. But the hand is coming.

R. The hand is forming, can you see it now it's forming. Can you see the fingers now? The fingers are coming towards Katie's hand. (*Katie quietly confirms each statement with a 'yes'*)

June. Keep it down, now.

Katie. Yes. Oh I can touch it. Oh I can. Oh, it's like a real hand!

80

R. Are they touching you?

J. It is a real hand! It is a real hand!

K. Oh! It's warm, it is warm!

R. Yes. Well that is what they do ... they come back as they are.   **K.** Oh. It's lovely!

R. Are they touching your hand now? That's good, Walter. *(June chips in 'yes he is')*   **K.** Yes, yes.

R. That's wonderful that, Walter. Touching your fingers, still touching your fingers? Is it going backwards now?

J&K. Yes. It is going back.

R. It is going back towards the medium. Well done, friends that was.... .**J.** Well done Walter.

K. That was an experience. /**R.** That was wonderful, Katie.

W. Ma'am, I hope that will be an experience that you will never forget. (**K.** I certainly won't.) - Of course it is warm and of course it is real for it is my hand ma'am!

R. Yes, that's right Walter.

W. Ok, Ok, Ma'am I ask you if you would remove your hand and return to your seat. (**K.** Thank you.)

(end of section 8)

Section 9   *(Track 9; Intro p44)*
Materialised Form.

This excerpt opens with indecipherable comments by the Circle.

Ray. He's come back out now.

June. Listen, someone's walking.

Katie. I can hear them!   **June.** Oh, wonderful.

Gaynor. Oh bless you friend. You are so welcome.

Materialised Form. My friends....

Ray. It's our friend again. 'The Voice'.

M.F. I must ask that you should all remain perfectly still.

Circle. We certainly will / There's a tapping.   **R.** Yes.

K. Oh, someone is touching my head.

Various voices. Lovely. / **Ray.** When you say....
K. Two hands on my head.
R. Two hands on your head. **K.** Oh, Thank you very much.
M.F. Bless you my child.
Katie. Thank you, thank you very much.
(other comments not decipherable)
June. Have you got them on yours, Mike?
Mike. Touching my hair.
Ray. One or two? One or two, Mike?
Mike. I'm not sure I think two. Yes, two.
Katie. Two are still on my head.
Ray. Are they still on your head?
K. Yes they are still on my head.
R. And are they on yours Mike?
Mike. They are still on my head, yes.
R./J. & others. That's superb. Bless you friends. / Two
people? / Yes. God bless you friends.
M.F. I would like you all to understand (R. Yes we're
listening) - that what we are doing here within this meeting
place between our worlds now is but nothing to what we
know we shall be able to do in time. (**Circle.** Yes, yes etc) It
is our intention, my friends, that soon we shall be able to walk
amongst you within the light. (**Circle.** Oh superb, that would
be wonderful. etc.) - We hope that we shall achieve this.
(indecipherable comments) - My Friends, all that we have done
here this evening we could not have done without the love
that you have brought here. **All.** Thank you.
Ray. You can take it all home with you.
J. He's still walking about.
K. Hands on my head again. Thank you.
M.F. Oh my child there is so much to be done.
K. Yes I understand.
M.F. You know... (**K.** I do. I'll do all I can.) You know my
love, and all the love of all those in my world involved in this

82

wonderful work, shall always be with you. (**K.** Thank you, thank you. I shall do all I can.) – We know and we understand. **K.** Yes. Thank you.
(circle make the comments undecipherable)   **K.** Thank you.
J.   Wonderful, friends, as always.
M.F. ...I find as always that the weight.... It is so difficult.
(circle comments drown out the last words)
G.   You've done well, friend.   **J.**   We appreciate that.
G.   You've done exceptionally well.
K.   He's got stronger as well.

(end of section 9)

Section 10   *(Track 10; Intro p44)*
Walter and matter through matter.

Walter. What I shall try to do now, hmm? Many folks in your world, in ignorance, many consider that this is no more than some kind of party trick. But then I would always reply that it is nothing of the sort, ma'am, hmm? It is merely an experiment, a small experiment, so that we can clearly demonstrate to you, ma'am, how close our two worlds truly are. What we can do when folks come together to sit in love and in harmony. When there is sufficient energy available, ma'am, you understand. (**Sue.** Yes I do.) – What I shall try to do now will be your experience but you must not keep this to yourself. You must take this experience out into your world so that you can share with your fellow men, hmm? (**Sue.** Yes. I shall.) – Ok. I want you to listen carefully to what I have to say, ma'am. I want you carefully to place your left hand in the hand of the medium, hmm? Oh, this is wonderful, ma'am; this is wonderful. (laughter) – This is a hand that I have not forgotten and shall not forget, ma'am, hmm? Ok, Ok. I want you now to understand that the medium is in a heightened state of sensitivity. You must do exactly as I ask. Place your right hand on top of your left ma'am. Move your right hand very gently up the arm of the medium so that you can feel the strap. Hmm? (**S.** Yes) - You can feel the strap ma'am? (**S.** Yes) - Move your hand away. You are holding Stewart's hand? (**S.** Yes) - The strap is there, ma'am? Feel again. (**S.** Yes) ..... Move your hand away.

(there is a sound like a short, sharp intake of breath)

June. What's happened, Sue?   **Sue.** It's freed.

W. Tell the folks what has happened, Sue.

Sue. The strap has completely broken away and the arm is now in the air.

W. You think that it has broken away, ma'am. Feel the arm of the chair. Is the strap there? (**S.** Yes, The strap's there) - Pull the strap hard. (**S.** Yep. I'm pulling it) - You have not let go of Stewart's hand for a moment. (**S.** No) - You havewitnessed the passage of living matter through matter, ma'am. Raymondo, switch on your light so that all may see.

R. Can you see it?   **Circle.** Goodness, yes, yes.

W. Now is that not something ma'am?

Sue. It certainly is......

(end of section 10)

Section 11   *(Track 11; Intro p45)*
Freda explains ectoplasm.

Katie. ... so many questions that they asked as well. They asked me, 'what is ectoplasm made of?'

Freda. Oh I'll tell you dear. I'll tell you. I think,... I wished that you'd asked this question of Walter 'cos his understanding is far greater than mine but I will do my best for you dear. (**K.** Thank you.) - Life itself is a trinity, dear. There is the physical, there is the spiritual body and then there is the mind. (**K.** Yes) - The physical body is that which you inhabit as you proceed along through life upon the earthly path. (**K.** Yes.) - But the life of the physical body is merely temporary, dear. (**K.** Yes.) - When you pass from the earth plane then your physical body returns to the earth but your spiritual body is an exact replica of your physical body. Within your spiritual body is your mind. I'm uncertain whether you have heard me say this before, Katie, but the mind is all that you are; all that you were and all that you will be. It is your personality; it is your complete memory. It is... it is you in totality, dear, but it is the eternal aspect of yourself for your spiritual body together with your mind will proceed on into eternity. It is indestructible, dear. Your physical brain is merely an instrument of the mind that is all. It is nothing in itself. But it gives physical expression to your mind, dear, the eternal aspect of yourself. You will therefore understand that there is physical matter and there is spiritual matter. (**K.** Right, yes.) - Between the two is a form of dynamic energy which we often refer to as ectoplasm for it is neither physical nor spiritual in nature; it is the only substance or energy which lies between the two states of existence. It is both spiritual and it is physical. (**K.** Yes.) - You understand what I am saying dear? (**K.** I think I do.) When you take part in a physical séance and we attempt to manifest in a physical manner (**K.** Yes.) - then we must take from the medium the energy, the vital energy, the substance, ectoplasm, and it is upon this that all physical phenomena rests and depends; without that there would be no physical contacts. It is between the two states of existence, unique to neither but common to both. You understand what I am saying, Katie? (**K.** I think so, yes.) - Ectoplasm can be manipulated by the - er- scientific people in my world in such a manner that its very nature can be changed. Its molecular structure can be changed from something that is almost smoke-like in appearance to something which is solid to the touch. (**K.** Right.) - It can be changed; it can be manipulated to something which is filmy, which is unsubstantial to something which is very substantial, that is solid to the touch. (**K.** Yes) - From the ectoplasm the scientific people are able to create what we often refer to as sss…either pseudopods or ectoplasmic arms it is these that are connecting themselves to the trumpets, dear. (**K.** Right.) - But the other end of the arm or the pseudopod must remain in contact with the medium for it is truly a part of the medium. (**K.** Right.) - It is a vital form of energy. We are then able to create….*(intake of breath)*- We are then able to change the structure of the arm from something which is invisible to something, on occasions, which is visible and it is this which will support and manipulate the trumpets. You understand, Katie? (**K.** Yes I do, yes.) - I think that you have seen photographs? (**K.** I have, yes.) - that is all it is, dear, I make it sound very simple… 'that is all that it is' it's very complex.

K. Yes. It's just when you are trying to talk to other people. Trying to explain to them.

Freda. I know, dear, but that's understandable, that's understandable, and that is precisely why ectoplasm is extremely sensitive to any form of light - it is rather like the photographer trying to develop his photographs in light - it cannot be done, dear. It has to be done the whole process within the darkroom. Life itself cannot be generated within light. It generates within darkness, within the womb of the mother, dear, and it is like an accelerated form of life itself. It is tthe birth of this form of energy but what takes 9 months….what takes 9 months to reach fruition is created in seconds within the séance room. You understand what I'm saying?

(**K.** I understand, yes, I understand.) - I know it is a great deal for you to understand, dear, and I'm doing the best that I can in the time that I have.

K. It does help. It will help me to explain it to other people.

F. Yes. And I say that if suddenly light is introduced within the séance room then the ectoplasm would return extremely quickly to the medium and this could create a haemorrhage, dear. (**K.** Right, yes.) - That is why it is dangerous. Physical mediumship, the exercising of physical mediumship is always dangerous. It has the danger - it has danger connected with it at all times and for precisely that reason most of the physical mediums in the past have chosen to work within the safety of their own séance rooms (**K.** I can understand that.) - within the safety of their own closed circles, where outsiders, where strangers have not been allowed within.

K. Yes. So in a way this explains why only the few people who know and see the ectoplasm.

F. Of course, of course, dear. We hope that this evening we shall be able to show ....Have you seen ectoplasm, dear?

K. I have, yes I have. Walter developed his hand.

F. But you have not seen it within the red light as it leaves Stewart? (**K.** No) - We hope that we shall be able to show you this evening, dear.

K. I've just seen it on top of the table.

F. Yes, where Walter was able to create his hand. What we hope to be able to show you this evening, you will see will be unaffected by the red light will appear as white - snow white. (**K.** Yes) - That'll be a wonderful treat, dear. (**K.** Yes, that'll be lovely because...) - Something else for you to see.

K. Yes, thank you, yes.

(end of section 11)

<u>**Section 12**</u> *(Track 12; Intro p45)*
Walter demonstrates ectoplasm in the light.

Walter. Ok, Ok. We shall try to fulfil a promise which we made earlier today.

Voices of circle. Oh yes /good/ OK Walter. *(A loud yawn is heard)* /The curtains are moving./ Yes/ Yes/ They are open again.

W. Folks, we shall endeavour to extract from the medium the energy ecto-plasm. (**Ray.** Ok, my friend, yes.) - In doing so we hope that we can make it visible to you. (**Mixed voices.** Thank you, Walter./Oh, wonderful) - as it moves, as it passes from the invisible to the visible state then you should be clear... able to clearly hear the transformation as it takes place.

Circle. Right, Walter/ Yes Ok, Walter.　　**W.** Ok, Ok.

Ray. We shall be listening intently, yes.

(sounds of laboured breathing)

Women's voices. I can hear a crackling noise./You can hear it now. /A crackling noise. / Yes. *('static'crackling sound heard)*

R. We did ask him once whether that was the energy actually coming out, you know, of the body of the medium and he said no it was actually transforming it from invisible to visible. Sort of like a charge within the particles.

Man's voice. It sounds like a trapped butterfly.

R. That's the first time I heard that one. *(Laughter)*

Various Voices. Sounds like bubbles in the bath/or Rice Crispies.

R. Yes. Now you don't want me to do anything at the moment, do you Walter? (**Walter.** No.) - You'll give me instructions , won't you?

Mike. I feel a lot of coldness. (**Circle.** Yes, /You can, yes.)

W. Michael, sir, you will indeed continue to feel a lowering of the temperature. Raymondo (**R.** Yes, sir.) - when we are able to give the signal that we want your light for a period of 2 seconds only and then off. (**R.** Ok, my friend.)

Woman's voice. Where shall we look?

Gaynor. Into the cabinet.　　**Ray.** Into the cabinet towards Stewart. Now, I won't move forward.

June & Gaynor. And I won't. I'll sit back/ and I'll sit back.

R. So what you want to be doing is looking at Stewart's face in the cabinet. Usually it comes from the nose or the mouth.

J.&G. And I'm sitting right back/ And I've got to concentrate. *(A tap is heard.)*

J. There you are, Ray. *(There is a swishing of the curtain.)* - See it?　　　　**Circle.** WOW! / It's wonderful wow!

J. See. That light's bright, isn't it, Ray.　　**G.** Yeah.

(There is a choking sound)

Woman's voice. W -ow!　　**G.** Ok, friend.

R. Are you alright there now, Walter?

G. Raymondo!　　**R.** Ok.

W. Yes,The light is too bright.　　**R.** Ok, Walter.

W. Were you all able to see?

Circle. Oh yeah!/Yes/beautiful./Awesome/like a great white beard/It's Fantastic, yes/like candy floss.

J. The light is bright isn't it, Ray?

R. I've turned it right down now.

J. You've turned it right down?　　(A tap is heard)

J. There you are Ray. *(The light is put on again)* - There you are, look!　　**Circle.** Oh! Wow!

R. I could still see it the second time; it was still there; it is just a question of getting this…..

W. Then let us see what else we can do.　　**All.** Ok, Walter.

(end of section 12)

Section 13　　　　　　　*(Track 13; Intro p46)*
Walter writes.

Walter. June, I want the pad and the pen upon the table. (**J.** Right, Walter) Let me see what else I can do. Hmm? Raymondo, switch up your light slightly.

R. Switch it down a bit?　　**J.** Up a bit he said.

G. Down.　**J.** No, up a little bit he said.　**G.** Sorry. Dozy!

W. That is fine. .　That is fine.

J. I've put the pad on the table for you, Walter, and the pen.

G. The light went up and down a little bit.

R. No, just the light went on and off a little bit.

J. Yes it did. **R.** Short connection somewhere.

J. Yes it's been travelling around a bit, hasn't it Ray?

(long yawn is heard.) **G.** Good Heavens!

J. It's been travelling around. Can you see the mass coming out - coming towards the pad?

G. Are they going to write something?

J. Yes, yes. They are picking up the pen.

(Clicking noises are heard as the recording tape changes)

G. I can see the pen moving.

J. It is, yeah, it is, yeah. Well done, Walter. You are doing all right there. **G.** I think they are going to write. Who's doing that? *(referring to the clicks)*

W. Ma'am, tell me how do I spell Katie?

K. Oh! K. (**W.** Yes) - A. (**W.** Yes) - T. (**W.** Yes) - I. (**W.** Yes) - E. (**W.** Yes)

J. Is that how you have spelt it, Walter?

W. That is fine. *(laughter from June. .* **J.** Well done, Walter)

K. Think it's marvellous, that.

J. It certainly is.

(another long yawn, as energy is taken from Gaynor)

Sounds of tearing and paper being crumpled hide Katie's comment

J. Makes you wonder how they tear it off with one hand, doesn't it?

W. Katie, ma'am, reach out, that is for you to keep.

K. Thank you. (**J.** Have you got it?) - Thank you very much, thank you. **W.** It is my pleasure.

J. Well done Walter, well done.

W. It is a small memento for you to keep for ever, ma'am.

K. Thank you, Walter, I shall treasure this.

J. You certainly will won't you. Well done.

(end of section 13)

90

Section 14   *(Track 14; Intro p46)*
Walter giving evidence to Katie and Christine.

Walter. Ok.Ok.Ok. Your mother brings her love to you both.
Christine. Oh, thank you, Mum, love.
W. Ok.Ok. Tell me something **(K.** Yes) - Did she......
What is this regarding ironing? Hmmm? **(Katie** Ironing?) -
Yes, was she particularly...**(Ch.** Yes) - careful? **(Ch.** Yes, yes.)
You know what I'm saying here? **(Ch.** Yes she was, yes.) She
says she's trying to bring some evidence to you of her
presence here this evening. She's saying that I must mention
this to you both. Hmmm?
Ch. I've been thinking of her while I've been ironing. Yes.
W. I hope therefore that this proves to you Chris how close
your loved ones, who are now in my world, - how close they
are to you all. **(Ch.** Oh bless them, I know.) - You send out a
thought and they receive, hmm? **(Ch.** Thank you, Mum. **K.**
Thank you.) - Ok, Ok, Ok. She's saying if only once again
she could hold you both. **(K.** That'd be nice. / **Ch.** That would
be lovely.) - But you know.... but you know that she still loves
you in the way that she always did.
Ch. Bless her.
K. She's always in our thoughts.
W. And you in hers ma'am. This is a time to rejoice!
Everyone. Yes.Yes.

(end of section14)

Section 15   *(Track 15; Intro p47)*
Christopher.

Christopher. All right. We've got somebody here as well by
the name of Hill. H-.I.-L -Hill. Is there somebody here who
recognizes the name of Hill H-I-L? **(Man's voice.** It could be
..... *(unrecognisable)* Does somebody recognize the name of

Ronald Hill. H-I-L?
K. Ronald Hill? It wouldn't be to do with Ena's? ....er....)
Christopher. I don't know who it's got to do with. There's a gentleman here this evening (**K.** Ena's first husband.) - who's expressing some concern for his wife, and he is telling me his name is Ronald Hill. (**K.** Yes.) - You know what this is about? (**K.** I do, yes.) - Bloody 'ell I'm good tonight, ain't I? (**Gaynor.** You are, aren't you!) - I'm surprising myself.*(laughs)* We're going to have a good night tonight!

(end of section 15)

Section 16 *(Track 16; Intro p47)*
Freda helping a communicator.

Freda. The gentleman who comes here this evening is telling me that his name is Ronald Hill, dear. Now he is connected with a lady friend of yours. (**Katie.** Yes, Georgina Brake.) - Yes. Now he's saying this, that he has tried for some time to reach her, dear, (**K.** Yes.) - and this he has done particularly during her sleep state. He has tried to reach out to her (**K.** Right.) - and you must know, dear, that he has been a little concerned in regard to her health, dear .(**K.** Yes) Now he's saying this .... and I'm not quite certain why, Ronald, you will not come and say this for yourself dear? I find this, Katie dear, to be such a nuisance. I would rather they come and speak for themselves. So I shall now allow him to come and speak, dear. (**K.** Ok.) - I must ask you to encourage him as much as you can and I'm sure that you will, dear. (**K.** Yes of course.) - Wait a moment.
K. Yes. Hello Ronald, Ron, Come on Ron,*(wheezy breathing is heard)* - Come and tell us what you have to say to Georgina.
Others. Come on friend /Come on, you can do it.
K. What have you got to say to George...Georgina?
Ron.*(rasping intake of breathe)* Oh, can (**K.** Hello.) - you hear

my voice?   **All.** We can hear you.

Ron.   I'm not certain whether .... how much I shall be able to do. I never knew you when I was on your side, but I do so want to take this opportunity to come here this evening .... Halliwell, Halliwell. (**K.** Halliwell, Yes, Katie.) - want to take this opportunity to come here this evening to thank you for all that you have done for my wife.

K. Ah, I thank you for what you have done and for what your wife has done. Is there anything I can pass on to her?

Ron.   Yes of course, of course. I want you to first of all to begin by telling her that I have taken this opportunity this evening to come to send my love, to send my love (**K.** I'll tell her, I'll tell her.) - you must also pass my love, my regards to Bob (**K.** Yes, I will.) - my dear friend, my dear friend. (**K.** Yes) - Tell him also that I am so delighted and so pleased and I have been for so many years now at the way in which - er-er - the life which they have been able to lead. You understand these words? (**K.** Yes, yes.) - I'm er-er-, what she has done, my darling, ... what my darling has done. She must know that I have been trying so hard to influence her from my side. (**K.** Yes. She'll understand.)

Ron. At last she has done it. She has put it down. She has left a record. That's all that really matters, she's left a record.

K. And important.

Ron.   Yes. Tell her that I am here with Chiefy. (**Ray.** - Chiefy?) (**K.** Chiefy, yes) - There's so many here .... there's so many here but tell her, tell her, that when the time comes I will be waiting. (**K.** I'll tell her, yes.)

Ron. It will be the three musketeers. (**Ray.** It'll be the three musketeers) - united at last. (**K.** Yes, that's lovely.) All my love. *(intake of struggling breathe)*

June/Gaynor. Ok/Ok, friend   **Ray.** Cheers Ron.

Ron. I can't manage any more.

Gaynor. You've done very well, very well.

K. Thank you Ron. I'll tell Ena and she'll listen to the tapes.

93

(sounds of kisses 'blown')

G. Kisses. That's lovely./ **Ray.** That was nice. / **J.**That's nice. / **G.** Well done.

K. Wonderful, lovely to help Ena

Ray. It must be, love.

J. Yes it will. Do her the world of good.

All. Ok, friend,..... come on, come on / You can do it /You're welcome.

Voice. I want ooo....   **Ray.** You want....?

Voice. I want to speak with my daughter. I want to speak with....   **J.&G.** Who's your daughter, friend?

Voice. It's Mam.   **J.&G.** It's Mum. Hello, love.

Katie. Hello.

Voice. It's Mum, Ooh yes!

Sitter. Who's mum are you? Katies?   **Katie.** Yes?

Voice. Oh. Aye. Oh, this is so wonderful, wonderful, wonderful

J. Wonderful, Katie.

K. Wonderful yes. I'm having a bit of difficulty hearing you

Voice. Oh I know, oh, I know oh, oh, oh,.....

K. Lovely to hear you, lovely to hear you...

Voice. My love, my love. *(choking gurgle)*

J. All my love, Katie, she said.   **K.** Well done.

Freda. Katie dear, (**K.** Yes Freda) - I have your mother here. She's sending her love to you.

K. She did very well.

F. Oh she did dear. Considering it's the first time. She was shouting so loudly...

K. Yes. I know it is difficult with my hearing.

F. That does not matter dear, that does not matter. Raymond (**Ray.** Yes) - This meeting, dear, everything that we are saying .... Ladies you'll be interested to hear this. I've said this before, Katie, but the ladies will be interested to hear that Raymond has a machine, dears, and everything that we say within this room, it goes within the machine so that at some time in the future, in many years from now, you will be able to hear my voice revolving around and around within the machine, dears, *(chuckles from the circle)*. (**J.** Wonderful isn't it?) - It's very technical and I'm not certain that I understand this myself but it goes round, dears. That's all that you need to know so you'll be able to listen to your mother's voice, dear. (**K.** Yes. I will, thank you). - She's sending her love to everyone. (**K.** Thank you) I find that I'm shouting, dears. (**All.** You are!) (**Ray.** We do agree with you tonight, HaHa !) (**J.** Is that 'cos it's breezy outside?) . It's for Katie, dear. It's for Katie. (**J.** I know, I know) - We are well aware of everything that you have done, dear. We are well aware of everything that you have done. (**K.** Right. Thank you) - and you'll be surprised at the outcome. (**K.** Right) - you understand what I am saying? (**K.** I do) - you'll be surprised at the outcome.

K. Yes   **J.** That'll be nice.

(end of section 16)

Section 17   *(Track 17; Intro p47)*
Freda gives evidence.

Freda. I have someone's husband here. Can you hear my voice?

Circle. Yes, we can hear.   **Ray.** We can hear you, Freda

F. I have someone hear who says that his name is Ted.

June. Ted?   *(A Voice gasps)*

Ray. Anyone accept Ted?   **June.** Who is that?

(someone calls Ola - Ola)

Freda. Ola dear, You remember when you sat here and Walter was speaking with you and he said then that he knew far more about you than you might imagine but the time was not right then for him to say…. It is my responsibility, dear. It is not for Walter. It is for me and I have your darling husband here, dear. (**Ola.** Thank you) - you can hear my voice? (**Ola.** Yes, thank you) Well we would like to make your evening, this evening, dear. We would like to make your year! Ola dear, your husband is so thrilled. Raymond, I want your light. June, I want you to change places with Ola. (**Ola.**Thank you)   (**J.** Come on, sit in my chair, dear.)   (**Ola.** Ok.) **Gaynor.** All right, friend.

F. Your husband would like to speak with you dear. You will understand that this will be far from simple but he will do his best. (**J.** (*aside to Ray*) Do you want this light on?) - Wait a moment. (**Ola.** Yes.)

J. Steady as you go friend, steady / **Ola.** Come on Ted (*Heavy breaths*)   **Ola.** Come on Ted

Ray.   Come on Ted, come on. This is good.
(*Everyone encourages him with 'Come on Ted'*)

Ted.(*heavy sigh*) Yes. Oh, how wonderful!

Ola. I've been longing to hear you

Ted. Yes, yes, how wonderful, how wonderful.(crying). (**A voice.** You're doing well) - I'm always with you. Always ! (**Ola.** Thank you. I know you are.) - Ohh. Give my love to..(gurgle)

June. Oh, he's gone bless him.   (**Ola.** Ohh!) - He did well.

Ray. It is so difficult for them

F.   Oh, he tried so hard dear. He certainly thinks such a great deal about you. He's saying that he came here and in many ways it was quite a surprise. (**Ola.** Yes.) - He's saying - like many others have said before him - that he did not want to leave, dear, he did not want to leave. (**Ola.** No, I know.) - I want to ask if a chicken means something to you? (**Ola.** A chicken? I don't think so.) - Is there someone here who knows something about a chicken? What a strange thing? (**Ray.** It is isn't it, yes.) - There is dear, and it applies to you. There is something concerning a chicken. (**Ola.** I'm not chicken.)   - What is it, dear?   (**Ola.** I'm not a chicken I said. I'm not frightened.) - Oh no, I don't mean that. (*laughter from the group*) - No, oh no. I mean the actual animal, dear. There is some connection - there is something to do with a chicken.

I'm not certain, I'm not certain… (**Ola.** Oh, I remember) - Well what is it?

Ola. I remember. When we were married - about four years …. my husband went out with some workmates and he got drunk and he lost the chicken. *(much laughter from everyone)* …. and I wasn't very pleased.

Freda. Then that explains, dear, why, when he said that, he was standing here with such a smile upon his face, saying, tell her about the chicken. Ask her about the chicken then she will know that it is me. (**Ola.** Yes it is. Definitely, definitely./ **Ray.** Good, good) - Well I want to tell you, dear, and I have to be serious for a moment, that your husband has forgotten nothing. His love for you today is as strong as ever it was when he was at your side. (**Ola.** Thank you.) - You must know that, dear. (**Ola.** I do know it.) - You must know that. (**Ola.** Yes. I do know it.) - And he's not in the photograph, dear. There is no point in kissing the photograph. *(laughter)* Do you understand what I'm saying? (**Ola.** Yes, I understand.) - There is no point. He's not there. He's with you whenever you send a thought out to him and he wants you to know how delighted and proud he is of you, dear. (**Ola.** Thank you very much. / **Ray.** Good.) - He's so proud. (**Ola.** He would be, I think.) - Oh, he is dear. It is not a question of he would be, he is dear. He is so delighted. From him to you, dear, I have to do this … *(sounds of kisses being 'blown')* (**J.** Ah, lovely) (**Ola.** Thank you.) - Just tell me - have you a small, this is quite a small glass container, this is very small. Two inches by inch and a half. (**Ola.** Yes, yes, yes.) - You know what I mean, dear. (**Ola.** Yes, yes) - It's a small glass receptacle of some kind.

Ola. He used to collect miniatures (**F.** I see) - I've still got it (**F.** I see) -a little bottle of beer. Two….

F. I see, I see, I see, I see. He knows all about that, dear. I'm surprised you never threw it away. (**Ola.** No, no, no, no, no) - Oh I see, keep it as a keepsake. (**Ola.** I've got 150 of them.)

Oh I see, dear. I see, I see, I see (**R.** We could all get drunk.) - Raymond, I want your light, dear. (**Ola.** Thank you very much.) - If you will kindly return to your seat. (**Ola.** Thank you very, very much.) - It is my pleasure dear and when you return home this evening you will now know within your heart and mind that truly your darling husband is always at your side, dear. (**Ola.** Yes, Thank you very much, thank you.) - Thank you dear.

J. Ok, Ola, Take you back, Take your time, no rush, alright?

Ola. - Yes, thank you.

Freda. I want to tell you all something, dears. We have an evening of Teds. Is there someone else here, whose husband is called Ted in my world? No? (**J.** Ted, nobody called Ted?) - I see.

Sitter. An ex. Ex-husband.

F. An ex-husband ? Is he in my world, dear?

Sitter. He certainly is.

F. He's here this evening. Does that surprise you?

Sitter. No, not really.

F. Oh, I see. He's here this evening. He's sending his love. (**S.** Bless him. Thank you.) - He's sending his love, dear. (**S.** Thank you.) - You know what has taken place and what has gone, has truly gone? You know what I'm saying dear?

(**Sitter.** I do exactly, yes.)-Have you a daughter,dear? (**S.** Er, Yes, I did have.) -Yes, in my world? (**S.** Yes) - because she is here also. (**S.** Thank you very much.) - is this his daughter? (**S.** Yes, it is.) - yes because they are here together, (**S.**- Thank you. -*becomes emotional*) - they are here together, dear. June, Raymond, I want your light. (**Ray** . Yeah, OK, Lovely.) - What is your name, dear?   (**Sitter.** It's that Sue again) - It's Sue again. Oh, come and sit here.

J. Come on Sue. We'll put the light on for you.

F. Come and sit here. (**R.** Lovely, lovely) - Give me your hand, dear. Oh yes, oh yes, I remember well. (**Sue.** Do you?) - Oh yes I do. (**S.** Thank you.) - I do, I do. These people have come here together (**S.** Yes I understand that.) - and your daughter has such great love for you, dear. (**S.** Bless her, thank you.) -She has such great love for you. (**S.** Thank you.) - Did you realize, did you understand, did you accept and did you appreciate that in her short life there was no one upon the Earth quite like you. (**S.** No I didn't appreciate that.) - Oh you, well I'm here to tell you this evening, dear, because she's telling me (**S.** Thank you.) - she's saying whatever, *whatever* the situation may have been. You understand what I'm saying? (**S.**- Exactly. Yes I know what you mean.) - deep within her heart, dear, (**S.** I know.) - unspoken words, (**S.** Yes thank you.) - and what a great shame, and I speak to you all now, dears. What a great shame it is that very often because we are humans, we find such great difficulty in truly expressing our emotions for a whole variety of reasons and some times we find life can be extremely cruel. We suddenly awaken one day to realize that it is too late. (**S.** Yes. That's right. Exactly. I know what you're saying.) - but listen everything that you have sent to her has reached her. (**S.** Thank you.) -You understand? (**S.** I do, I do, yes.) - everything has reached her, dear. (**S.** Thank you very much.) - she's saying that in the past she has wanted so much to come to you, oh yes, but the time has never been right but this evening perhaps because of all the love and energy available within this room. There is not a mother within this room, dear, that does not feel for you at this moment in time (**S.**Thank you very much.) - and I can say that because I myself, I am a mother also (**S.** Really? Right.Thank you.) - Oh yes. oh yes, oh yes. But he is saying that he has her. (**S.** Good.) - Do you understand? (**S.** and that is the way it should be.Yes) - Yes, he has her (**S.** Thank you) - but he is her father and you are her mother. (**S.** that's correct) -nothing will ever change that, dear. **S.** Bless you, thank you.) - nothing will ever change that. (**S.** Thank you.) - You know that she is always with you, Sue? (**S.** Thank you) - She is always with you. (**S.** Lovely, thank you) Do you know something about a ribbon, dear?

Sue. Doesn't spring to mind at the moment.

F. There is something about a ribbon.

Sue. I used to wear ribbons when I was little and hated them.

F. Let me ask (**S.** Huh, hmm) Do you know someone by the name of Doug, - Douglas or Duggie? (**S.**Yes.) - Is this in my world or is he still in your world? (**S.** In the Earth plane, Earth plane.) - There is some connection here and I'm not certain what this is. Is this someone who you have spoken to? I'm speaking of in recent times. (**S.** er. No not recently, no.) - No, in the last few months. No? (**S.**No, not really, no.) - Oh I see.

Sue. There may be a Duggie in the Spirit World. I've lost contact with him 20 years ago. (**F.** Oh I see.) - A friend of my father. (**F.** I see, I see) - He was Doug, Duggie.

F. I see, I see, I see. Because you were a pretty little thing, dear (**S.** I was, yes) (*other laughter*) - You still are. Forgive me, forgive me. You still are, dear. (**S.** Oh, you are sweet.) - O, well, I suddenly realised what I said. (**S.** Thank you.) - but as a little girl you were extremely pretty (**S.** Was I?) - and one of the recollections that this person has of you, was ribbons in your hair (**S.** Oh yes.) - This is what it is, dear (**S.** Oh yes I was young then, much younger, that was it.) - You're still a darling (**S.** *laughs* -Thank you.) - So again, when you leave here, Sue, you will know your darling daughter has been for you this evening. (**S.** I certainly will. Thank you.) - Would you know who Helen is, dear? (**S.** I would have called her Helen) - You would? I see. Because that is the name that she has. (**S.** Thank you. I asked that question. Thank you.) - You have. People sometimes tend to forget that very often communication exists upon an emotional level, on a mental level sometimes the unsp.... People do not need to speak, sometimes we are able to receive directly from their minds what they wish to say and yes, Eric is here. (**S.** That's my Dad. Yes he is. (**S.** Thank you. Thank you./**Ray.** Oh lovely.) - He is here for you this evening. (**S.** Thank you.) - He is here for you this evening. It is him that is speaking of the ribbons, dear. (**S.** Oh he would.) - Yes he's speaking of the ribbons. You were always his little girl, dear. (**S.** Yes I know that.) - You were always his little girl and you still are. (**S.** Oh, I love him. Thank you.) - One day..... One day in the future you will all be together again (**S.** Yes, I know, I know, thank you.) - I think we've had quite a reunion, dears, this evening.

Many voices. Oh yes. We have, we have, thank you.) *(laughs of pleasure)*

F. It's been wonderful. Raymond I want your light. Sue dear, if you'd be so kind.....I want to say one further thing. I want to ask. I want to impress this upon people. I understand that people are people. I understand this so I want you Sue, if you will, to announce aloud that everything that you have just been given, by me, that Stewart knew absolutely nothing about it whatsoever.

Sue. No, no, nothing at all. We met briefly two months ago that's all. (**F.** Yes, yes.) - and just shook hands, that's all.

F. Because I would hate for anyone to leave here and think, but perhaps Stewart knew the lady? (**S.** Definitely not.) - He does not, dears. (**Many.** He does not./ No, no.) - He does not. And I'm only saying that because I want you all to realise, to accept and embrace this great truth.

Ray. Yes, yes.

Molly. Freda, we've had wonderful evidence from you. (Agreement from others)

F. Oh you are very kind, dear. (**S.** Molly is kind.)

F. You're very kind. She's a sweet lady (**S.** She's lovely.) (**Molly.** Person!) - Molly we do, we do appreciate all that you do. You must understand that, dears. (**M.** Ok,Ok) - we appreciate all that you do.

(end of section17)

Section 18   *(Track 18; Intro p48)*
Freda speaks about acceptance of the 'Truth'.

Katie. One of the questions that people ask is 'why isn't this general knowledge, why is it only a few that know about the Spirit and the afterlife?'

Freda. I think Katie that the best way that I can answer that is in this manner. That there are only a very small percentage of the population of the Earth who express an intelligent interest in these things, but is it not strange that most of the population of your Earth even though they will speak in ignorance, with a total lack of knowledge or understanding, will proffer opinions which they cast in stone as *great truths*, (**K.** Yes.) when really they are merely speaking with a total lack of understanding or knowledge. (**K.** Yes.) For you who have taken the time, for you who have taken the trouble, to investigate for your self, for you who know the truth then it is not, I would say - it will never be, fruitful to speak to those who have already made up their minds and based their understanding and opinions upon nothing but biased personal beliefs. (**K.** Yes.) - What other subject upon the Earth would someone chose to elaborate upon if they had no understanding? (**K.** Yes.) - There is none, dear. (**K.** No.) Only on this matter of the nature of life that everyone suddenly has a wonderful opinion.

K. Yes. It is interesting to hear your point of view because I'm trying to help these people and there is so much magic happening that they think 'Oh there must be ways of doing this', because magicians are so clever and do all sorts (**F.** Oh yes, dear, we have heard this.) - and you hear all sorts of that, what they're thinking of, (**F.** Oh yes, dear.) - and it is difficult to express the truth.

F. And of course one has to bear in mind also that in the past there have been so many, what Walter often refers to as 'pseudo-mediums', those who profess to be mediums who are nothing of the sort. Many of these are deceiving themselves. You understand what I'm saying, Katie? (**K.** Yes.) Many believe themselves to have the gift when in reality they have merely - they will be exercising an overactive imagination, (**K.** Yes.) - that is all. Then we have those mediums who have perpetrated, and I use the word because there is none other that will express what I am trying to say here; there are those who have operated in a fraudulent sense. We all know of these. We know their history, dear, but there are always and have always been quite excellent mediums and it's these that you hear so little about. (**K.** Yes.) People forget them. People say all Spiritualists are frauds, all mediums are frauds. Well, that is rather like saying that because there is one bad apple in a basket, dear, that all the apples must be bad. There are within your - there are within your police force those, from time to time, who behave in a dishonest manner (**K.** Yes.) - but that does not mean to say that all of your police force are dishonest. It merely means that a very small percentage are. And so it is within Spiritualism and within Mediumship, there will always be those who produce fraud in an unconscious or in a conscious sense but then equally there will always be those who are quite genuine.

K.   Yes, yes.

F.   There is so much ignorance, Katie.

(end of section 18)

Section 19

(Track 19; Intro p48)

Walter talks to Katie.

Walter.   I would like to begin today by saying something which I believe is extremely important, hmm? (**Katie.** Yes.) - If I at any time should say anything that you are unable to hear then I would like you to stop me, ma'am. (**Katie.** I will, yes.) - Ok, Ok, Did you know …may I call you Katie?

K. Katie, yes.

W. Fine, you may call me Walter, ma'am. (**K.** Ok, Walter, thank you.) - Did you know that here are many souls in your world, particularly those who call themselves Spiritualists who believe that we who choose to return and work in this manner are in some way elevated spiritual souls? They believe that we are filled with great spirituality. (**K.** Yes.) - I can tell you, ma'am, that this is poppycock. Hmm? (**K.** Yes.) - I want you to clearly understand, for this is important, (**K.** Yes.) - whilst there are indeed those who return in this way; who choose to return in this way; who enjoy opportunities *(heavy breath)* - to instruct, to advise, to inform, to educate people as to the true nature of life; there are those who do return so that they may fill those who come here with great spirituality; those who will share their spiritual knowledge. (**K.** Yes) - There are those who will do so, visitors from my world, workers from my world (**K.** Yes.) but that is not the purpose of our work through Stewart. Hmm. (**K.** Right.) - It is merely so that we can share with you the wonderful truth, the wonderful reality of life beyond death and of communication between our two states that we should from time to time be able to reunite those who come here, with their loved ones who now reside in my world. That is the nature and the purpose of the work that we undertake through Stewart. Hmm? (**K.** Yes.) - Ok, Ok, It is important, Katie, that all who come here should understand. So we want you today to think of us not as some great spiritual souls but as fellow human beings, for that is what we are ma'am. (**K.** Yes) - We are a little further along the path of life but we still occupy, we all occupy, the whole of mankind; we all occupy the same path of life. Only we have progressed a little further upon that road (**K.** Right) - than what you have and that is the only difference, ma'am. (**K.** Yes) - Perhaps, because we have passed through the change called death our perspective on life is a little larger, a little broader than what yours might be but other than that, that is all, ma'am. (**K.** Yes) - Ok, I'm delighted that you are here today. You are a kindly soul and you have great work to do on behalf of my world, ma'am. Hmm.

K. Thank you yes.

(end of section 19)

Section 20   *(Track 20; Intro p49)*
The Spirit Team says 'Goodnight' - July 8th 1999.

Walter. Ok, Ok, Folks, I cannot hold on (**Sitters.** Thank you, thank you, Walter.) - and I wish to thank each and everyone of you for your love and for making our coming together this evening possible. You are kindly souls and we bring and leave with you our eternal love. Good night folks.

Sitters. Goodnight, God bless./Good night, thank you./ God bless you./ That was wonderful.

June. Hello, Freda, (**Ray.** Hello Freda.) - We're with you Freda. Just take it steady.

Ray. We're here, Freda We're still here Freda. (**J.** Take our love) - We've nearly melted away but we're still here. *(It had been an extremely hot day.)*

Freda. As I can see, Raymond, I can see. (**Ray.** and I've lost weight) - Dears, we need to bring this meeting to a close. I regret, Nicholas, Robert, I regret that because of the conditions here this evening it would not be possible for Stewart to give a private séance. (**N&R.** We understand.) - I think you will well understand, dears, (**N&R.** We do, thank you.) - but we would so like to be able to do that on some occasion in the future (**N&R.** It's been arranged.) - but with your wisdom and your knowledge you will understand. (**N& R.** Yes precisely.) - Goodnight to you all, dears.

All. Goodnight Freda/Goodnight to you./Thank you.

June. It is a bit hot, Ray, isn't it?

Christopher. Yesh... (**Ray and All.** Hello, Christopher. Nice for you to pop back.) (**J.** Oh it's lovely. ...) (**Ray.** I know you've only popped back, 'cos it's too warm.)
Chris. Yesh, I've got to go now, (**All.** Bye.) Can I just give my love to everybody? (**All.** Yes/All our love to you.) - Yesh, yesh, I'll see you all again won't I? (**All.** Yes. I hope so.) - All right. I love you all. Bye-bye.
J. God Bless.

White Feather. May the Great White Spirit be with you all.
June/Ray. And with you White Feather.. Goodnight, God Bless. Thank you very much.

(end of section 20)

Availability of books:-

'Experiences of Trance, Physical Mediumship and Associated Phenomena', Part One: Evidence of Survival After Death. ISBN 978-0-9514534-8-3 and its CD.

'Experiences of Trance, Physical Mediumship and Associated Phenomena', Part Two: Home Circles & Public Sittings. (Revised Edition) ISBN 978-0-9557050-2-1 and its double CD pack

All the above are available by contacting:-
'The Alexander Project'
at rjlister001@rjlister001.karoo.co.uk

Books without the CDs are available from:-
www.amazon.com & amazon.co.uk

'Life After Death - Living Proof' by Tom Harrison ISBN 978-0-9557050-1-4 is available from www.amazon.com and www.amazon.co.uk.
Or by contacting Tom at:- snppbooks@yahoo.co.uk.

Note:- Should any reader of this book ever choose to sit with the medium Stewart Alexander, they do so with the understanding that both parties recognise the experimental nature of the sitting, that expected results cannot be guaranteed, and that both parties are participating of their own free will.

Lightning Source UK Ltd.
Milton Keynes UK
29 December 2010

164962UK00009B/67/P